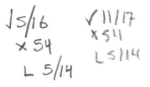

PLAN AND MAKE YOUR OWN

FENCES & GATES, WALKWAYS, WALLS, & DRIVES

E. Annie Proulx

Rodale Press, Emmaus, Pa.

#le⁵

Illustrations by Roberta Greene
Interior design by Linda Jacopetti
Photography by Rodale Press Photography Department and Jim Collins

Library of Congress Cataloging in Publication Data

Proulx, Annie.
    Plan and make your own fences and gates, walkways, walls and drives.

    Includes index.
    1. Garden structures—Design and construction—Amateurs' manuals. 2. Driveways—Design and construction—Amateurs' manuals. I. Greene, Roberta.
II. Title.
TH4961.P77   1983   643'.55   82-24120
ISBN 0-87857-452-2 hardcover
ISBN 0-87857-453-0 paperback
2   4   6   8   10   9   7   5   3   1   hardcover
2   4   6   8   10   9   7   5   3   1   paperback

CONTENTS

GIVE IN TO THE URGE TO ARRANGE AND IMPROVE

One of the most satisfying and irresistible aspects of gardening is to plot out bowers, terraces and courtyards, to look over a tangle of brush and weeds and envision in its place a brick walkway winding through perennial borders or an intricately knotted herb garden, to construct trellises and arbors for grapevines and climbing roses, or to fence in a tidy orchard where once there was only rough ground. The gardener's instinctual urge to arrange and improve his or her grounds for greater privacy, convenience or beauty is strong, but too often the tasks of building a solid stone wall or putting up a fence that won't fall over seem formidable and complicated jobs that only expert craftsmen should attempt. Fortunately, this is not true. All of the projects in this gardener's workbook are fairly simple and straightforward, even for those of us who are not particularly deft in construction techniques. The basic projects described here allow gardeners to translate their daydreams and imaginary garden plans into reality. The author knows well the lure of do-it-yourself landscaping projects: in more than 20 years of gardening, she has wrestled with collapsed stone walls and built new ones; made patios of brick and flagstone; constructed walks, terraces and driveways; and built picket fences. There is a kind of patient pleasure that grows out of working with stone, brick and wood, in seeing a beautiful garden emerge from an ugly backyard.

The projects in this book are useful to the suburban and small-yard gardener as well as the country resident with rolling acres. None of them are weekend quickies. Most take thought, contemplation and time, an approach to things familiar to anyone who has ever worked with growing plants and the soil, and are as soothing and relaxing to work at as gardening itself. A stone wall of body and size, for example, can take years to complete. An enormous wall that runs along the road of a small New Hampshire town not far from Mount Washington is 4 feet wide, as many feet tall, and runs for miles and miles along the fields. It must have taken a generation to build.

Some of the materials will appeal to you more than others. I have a particular fondness for fieldstone, but a friend of mine takes a mad delight in the possibilities lying in a heap of uncleaned brick, while another is the proverbial pig in clover when he gets his hands on boards, hammer and saw. This book is meant to encourage gardeners to undertake some construction projects themselves rather than call in an expensive contractor, or at least to understand what keeps stone walls from collapsing, gates from sagging or driveways from eroding if another must do the work. Working on grounds and garden improvement projects sharpens your eye for the details of topography and outdoor space, and will give you inordinate pleasure in the products of your own hands.

1

FENCES AND GATES

plus Trellises, Arbors and Pergolas

CHAPTER 1

THE FENCING-IN OF AMERICA

When the early settlers sailed across the Atlantic to the New World, they brought along with them some new agricultural attitudes, sprung from the breakdown of the old communal village land-holding traditions. The new trend was toward enclosure of individually owned land by fence, ditch or hedge, and the use of that land to suit the owner rather than the common good. Although early North American settlements were communal in nature and generally had common lands, the move toward private land holdings marked off with fenced and walled boundaries went inexorably forward over the decades.

The common fencing projects of our early days seemed to be a necessity. As the new immigrants poured in—20,000 people came to the American colonies in the decade between 1630 and 1640—bringing sheep, cows, hogs, goats, poultry and other livestock, and set to work planting vegetable gardens and orchards as fast as they could, the need for fences both common and private was a major pressure. Rough, hasty fencing was thrown up as fast as possible; no one had time to wait for hedges to grow.

Common fields were fenced in as soon as they were cleared, and the whole village worked together to put up the new fence. Every villager was then held responsible for keeping his share of the common fence in good repair. The town fence viewers—important and powerful men in early days—made sure all townsmen kept up not only the common fences, but also the fences around their individual gardens and orchards. Later, fence viewers could impose penalties and stiff fines for failure to mend fences, could dictate the rebuilding of an inadequate fence or sub-standard parts of it, could say of what materials and how the fence must be made, and could and would set the time when the fence had to be finished. Every town had its fence viewers, although in some places they were known as "haywards" from the Old English "hedge wards," a traditional office in England for at least four centuries, where tightly knit hedges of briar, ash, hawthorne, oak and alder made stock-proof boundaries between fields.

The major problem suffered by the colonists seemed to be animal trespass, rather than skulking Indians and privation. In those days, animals were fenced out, and the proliferating stock roamed, grazed and rooted where it would, leaping or digging into gardens and devouring precious rows of young vegetables grown from seeds carried across the Atlantic, or bursting into grain fields and gobbling voraciously. Even dogs and cats were a problem, for the early gardens were fertilized with buried fish, and dogs and cats, lured by the odor of decay, would dig up the putrefied fish, scattering seedlings and sprouts in all directions. Complaints, lawsuits for damages, unneighborly rancor, and

English Hedges

Thousands of miles of living hedges, spiky, impenetrable walls of woven branches, stems, stakes and withes, are a natural part of the English countryside. Some ancient hedges date back to Saxon times. Historians are able to date hedges by the number of shrub species they contain—roughly one new shrub species for every century of its existence. Thirty yards of medieval hedge today has about seven kinds of shrub in it. In the fifteenth and sixteenth centuries English land was increasingly enclosed, passing from common land to private land. There were many instructions to farmers on how to make hedges and dikes. One such idea was a kind of forerunner of the modern seed-tape: the farmer was advised to twist straw into a loose rope into which were worked the seeds of ash, hawthorne and oak. He was then to bury the length of rope where the hedge was wanted.

Hedges usually went with dikes, and keeping the one trimmed and the other scraped clear took a tremendous amount of labor, not just once a year, but several times, for generations and centuries. A good farmer took considerable pride in his well-laid hedges, and spent much of the winter with a billhook, slashing, twisting, staking and bending over the partially severed trunks of shrubs grown too large. Such chopped and twisted stems would put up thick shoots the next year, to be twined, in their turn, into the fabric of the hedge.

One of the most daunting designs was the "Galloway hedge," used extensively in Scotland in the eighteenth and nineteenth centuries. This combination of hedge, dike and stone wall was intended to impress that determined climber, the black-faced sheep.

As beautiful and as complementary to the landscape as hedges are, they are dying out in England, replaced by cheap and relatively movable barbed wire and electric fences. Expense isn't the only reason for the hedge's decline—social mobility and fewer farmers mean less hedging. It is an enclosure technique best suited to a tradition-bound society where change comes but slowly, and where continuing generations of farmers will keep them maintained.

If you wish to know more about hedging and how to do it, one of an excellent series of English booklets describes and illustrates the process: *Fields, Hedges and Ditches,* by Nigel Harvey, Shire Album 21, Shire Publications, 1976, Cromwell House, Church Street, Princes Risborough, Aylesbury, Bucks, U.K. You may order this through your bookseller.

village livestock pounds jammed with someone's errant stock represented a coarse, irritating thread in the fabric of colonial life. Any planting had to be protected from the wide-ranging animals. In 1653, for example, one Thomas Minor of New London, Connecticut, planted a clover patch, and to protect it, hammered 500 palings into the ground around it for a fence. Later generations of farmers would describe the ideal fence as "horse-high, bull-strong, and skunk-tight," but by that time, stock was fenced in, not out, and the free-ranging days were gone. Proper fencing was now serious business and fast became a community concern.

Town Meeting Day set the date for fence mending to be finished—usually in the spring. The tradition lasted long in Vermont, where the second week in May was the time to repair fences. This chore had to be done before mid-May when the cows were turned out to pasture, and fencing fit comfortably into the slack time between sugaring off and spring plowing. Fields and roads were still wet with rain and snow run-off, a period still called "mud season," when farmers, muttering that the trail to the woodlot was still too soft to use, squelched through the cold mud and mended fence and wall.

Often the town selectmen or the timber warden gave permission to cut timber from the common woodland for fencing in early times, and generally there was no lack of material to make fences. The traditional hedges and ditches of England took years to grow and dig, and the stone walls of New England, later so popular, were the products of slow field clearing, stone accumulation and off-season labor. The rapidly expanding colonial world demanded faster fencing techniques. Hence fences of stumps, brush, pales, logs, pickets and rails were put up as fast as they could be.

The height and maintenance of fences varied considerably from town to town. For example, in 1647, in Watertown, Massachusetts, a fence had to have four rails; six years later that requirement was refined to a specified height of 3½ feet. In its early days the town of Guilford, Connecticut, set fence heights at 4 feet, but in only a few years lifted heights to 4½ feet. By the last quarter of the seventeenth century most towns, sadder and wiser through unpleasant experience, insisted on 5 feet as a minimum fence height, and specified at least five rails for all fences around the temptations of corn field, garden and orchard.

The crudest of all fences, characteristic of new settlements as the frontier expanded in the United States and Canada, were piles of brush heaped high and wide, and the grotesque, menacing shapes of upturned tree roots. The stump fences, as the lines of roots were called, were somewhat reminiscent of the ancient military abatis, a fortification made of downed trees, the ends of the branches slashed into sharp points, piled together with the bristling points facing the enemy.

Brush fences looked formidable, but pigs rooted through them and large stock burst through by brute force and determination. Still, brush fences were easy to build. Since the brush and slash from land clearing had to be piled somewhere, why not use it as a temporary fence until there was time to build something sturdier? But in a short time brush fences were declared illegal in most towns, except in one Canadian township where it was decreed that a legal brush fence "must be forty feet wide and damned high."

Stump fences were another by-product of clearing land for cultivation. It wasn't enough to cut down the trees—the stumps had to be pulled; they could be disposed of and the new field fenced in one operation by dragging the stumps to the edges of the cleared area. Rarely did a person stump out a field and build the fence single-handed. Stumping bees involved all the neighbors and several ox teams in dislodging the huge stumps. The stumps and the roots below made a massive fence 12 to 15 feet high. First, the soil all around the stump would be dug and loosened, then all the spreading roots that could be reached (except for the hidden tap root) would be chopped through with axes. At last the oxen were hitched to the pulling chains in teams, each owner standing by his oxen to urge them forward, and on the sig-

nal they strained and pulled until slowly the great stump heaved from the earth and was dragged to the sidelines to guard the soil that once had nurtured it.

Although brush and stump fences continued to be built in new settlements for generations to come, in more established areas where the work of generations accumulated, four basic types of fence became common, and all but one of them are still familiar to the North American landscape.

Pale Fence Palings were tall saplings, split or whole, and a paling fence was simply the sharpened ends of hundreds of palings driven deep into the ground. The top was given stability by using withes (bands made of slender, flexible twigs) or tough vines to tie the palings to a pole top-rail. The fence maker could take his material from the woodlot with only an axe for a tool, and pound the palings into the ground with the heel of the same implement. The cost was nothing but his labor and the future emptying of the woodlot.

Picket Fence Sturdier, more versatile, and more attractive than the paling fence was the picket fence, which came into existence only when sawn lumber was available. The early picket fences weren't painted, and were often set with a kickboard along the bottom to keep out the snuffling, ubiquitous hogs that roamed the streets. Their primary function was to keep stray livestock out of yards and gardens. A single diagonal cut at the top made a threatening-looking fence that most animals would think twice about before trying to jump over.

Log Fence Log fences were heavy, massive structures built by community labor like laying up a log house or barn; strong spirits made the work go forward. Some of these huge fences were built with 60-foot-long logs, and used tremendous amounts of straight trees. Such fences were called "bull-nay" for their strength to withstand the most obstreperous bull—they were intended to hold strong, dangerous animals. Log fences are rarely seen today.

Rail Fence The most common fence of all, in those halcyon days of fast-growing, straight-splitting chestnuts and rich stands of fence timber, was the rail fence. Scores of variations have been recorded, but two favorites were the straight-line post-and-rail, and the Virginia zig-zag rail, also called a "worm" or "snake" fence. The zig-zag fence and the variant stake-and-rider fence were easier to build than the post-and-rail, and called for only an axe and a mattock for a little shallow digging. The strength of the worm fence came from the criss-crossed rails at the intersections and the zig-zag shape. But there were drawbacks to this picturesque structure; it took a tremendous number of rails, covered considerable land (from 6 to 30 percent of a field fenced by zig-zag was "fence-waste"), and harbored weeds and brush and hungry wildlife in the uncountable corners. European eyes, accustomed to the charm of ancient hedges dividing properties, found these proliferating fences less than attractive. At the end of the eighteenth century, French philanthropist and writer La Rochefoucauld-Liancourt complained of "these eternal fences of dead wood which greatly disfigure the landscape," and advised Americans to plant hedges.

It was not aesthetics which turned fence makers from the zig-zag to the straight post-and-rail, but a dwindling supply of fence timber. In 1763 farmer John Bartram from the Philadelphia area wrote "what our people will do for fencing and firewood fifty years hence I cannot imagine."

It was a good deal more work to make a mortised post-and-rail fence than the old zig-zag. Chestnut, locust and red cedar made good posts, and trees with a diameter of about one foot were felled, cut into 6- or 8-foot lengths, then split in half with a maul and wedge. The post section intended to stand above ground was mortised every 4 to 6 inches; first holes were bored with an auger, then the holes were neatly shaped with hammer and chisel. In the nineteenth century there were special machines available just to bore out post mortises. Since these contraptions were too expensive for one farmer to own, they were often community purchases in some regions. The finished posts were set in a straight line every 9 or 10 feet. The rails were usually of chestnut for its decay resistance and easy splitting characteristics, but oak and ash were used too. The standard rail length was and still is 11 feet. Large straight trees of good rail quality were downed, cut into 11-foot lengths, then split into 8 to 16 rails, a task that took considerable skill. A good rail-splitter, in 1825, could get 50 cents per hundred rails, with his board provided. By 1869 the rate was up to 18 cents for each rail.

The rail and the picket fence are our indigenous fence styles, part of the traditional rural North American landscape, but after the mid-nineteenth century the rail fence began to decline, and many fine old fences ended in the woodshed, replaced in the field by barbed wire.

There were a few spasmodic attempts in the milder sections of the East to replace wooden fencing with hedges, but American farmers couldn't quite get the knack of it, though considerable hedging was grown on the New Jersey coast and in the plains states where timber was scarce before barbed wire swept all other fencing away. As late as 1887 George Martin, in his useful manual, *Fences, Gates and Bridges,* was recommending osage orange *(Maclura pomifera)* for living hedges where they wouldn't interfere with land sub-divisions, as around an apple orchard. Nurserymen made a good living propagating osage orange and selling the small plants for hedging. Remarks Stevenson Fletcher in his monumental *Pennsylvania Agriculture and Country Life, 1640–1840:*

> Those who used it regretted their choice; it was viciously thorny, occupied much land, required much soil moisture, and took much time to keep within bounds. Including labor, it cost as much or more than a post-and-rail fence. Most farmers did not keep it trimmed.

Barbed wire—that ugly, efficient, inexpensive fencing material—changed the shape of agriculture, transformed the ways and manners of the Old West, and wiped out thousands of miles of cover, food and habitat for birds, small animals and indigenous prairie plants holding out against the cow and the plow. The shelter offered the native flora and fauna against rail fences and hedges was reduced to the thin shadow as fine as a pen line cast by the unrolling miles of iron wire.

The first patent for barbed wire was taken out in 1867 by William D. Hunt, a New Yorker, but other barbed wire inventors were hot on his heels, and by the 1870s they were beginning to turn the stuff out at a tremendous rate in the new barbed wire center of the world, DeKalb, Illinois. In a ten-year period—from 1874 to 1884—the amount of single-strand barbed wire in use jumped from 10 miles of wire to 250,000 miles! It was a revolution in fencing. Even in the East where timber was still relatively plentiful, farmers switched to barbed wire because it was cheap, faster and easier to put up, and took up less land than post-and-rail. When the chestnut blight hit shortly after the turn of the century, this best of fencing material gradually disappeared, removing the most practical alternative to barbed wire from the farmers' woodlots.

In this century barbed wire has moved over for the even flimsier electric fence, a ridiculously fragile wire stretched between skinny pickets, its white, ceramic insulators visible from far across the fields, like vacant, moronic eyes in the landscape.

Edmund Cody Burnett, in his 1948 "Passing of the Old Rail Fence," waxed nostalgic as he wrote:

> In the good old days when the rail fence reigned supreme, the farmer could take his secure and fairly comfortable seat on the top rail, smoke his corn-cob pipe and survey his farm, thoughtfully laying plans for the future. When a neighbor came over, as neighbors often did, the two would sit on the fence, whittle, smoke, and hold unhurried discourse. . . . There never was a finer school for agricultural, civic and political training than the old rail fence.

Stevenson Fletcher quotes this idyllic passage in his 1955 work *Pennsylvania Agriculture and Country Life, 1640–1840,* but adds his own sharp-elbowed dig at modern fencing—"Nowadays farmers cannot be even fairly comfortable sitting on their barbed wire or electric fence to smoke, whittle, or neighbor."

Thinking about Fences

The kind of fencing you choose for your own place involves much more than simply picking out the style and the materials, as when choosing wallpaper; you'll search for a fence that goes harmoniously with the architecture of your house and that fits the depth of your purse; you'll also look for local fencing material. But the climate, the prevailing neighborhood style of fencing (which can range from New England picket to California redwood grapestake), even your neighbor's taste, will count in the choice.

If you have a city roof or penthouse garden, a small movable screening fence like a woven wattle hurdle will break the skyscraper winds

Lost Prairie Flowers

Aldo Leopold wrote in *A Sand County Almanac* about the disappearance of one prairie plant.

> Every July I watch eagerly a certain country graveyard that I pass in driving to and from my farm. It is the time for a prairie birthday, and in one corner of this graveyard lives a surviving celebrant of that once important event.
> It is an ordinary graveyard, bordered by the usual spruces, and studded with the usual pink granite or white marble headstones, each with the usual Sunday bouquet of red or pink geraniums. It is extra-ordinary only in being triangular instead of square, and in harboring, within the sharp angle of its fence, a pin-point remnant of the native prairie on which the graveyard was established in the 1840's. Heretofore unreachable by scythe or mower, this yard-square relic of original Wisconsin gives birth, each July, to a man-high stalk of compass plant or cutleaf Silphium, spangled with saucer-sized yellow blooms resembling sunflowers. It is the sole remnant of this plant along this highway, and perhaps the sole remnant in the western half of our country. What a thousand acres of Silphiums looked like when they tickled the bellies of the buffalo is a question never again to be answered, and perhaps not even asked.

and give you some privacy from staring faces in adjoining buildings. In suburbia or a town neighborhood, a high, sturdy board fence can give a badly needed sense of solitude to the garden, can keep neighbors, their dogs and their children out of view, and can conceal unsightly oil tanks, garbage cans or a garage entrance. These big privacy fences can also muffle blatting motorcycle exhausts, mark property boundaries and function as a backdrop for espaliered pear trees or a foaming waterfall of Silverlace. The depressing long lines of adjoining back yards in suburbia, each with its plastic wading pool and boring stretch of shaved lawn, are a kind of garden slum when measured against the infinite possibilities presented by fences that enclose secret gardens, that foster peacefulness and an individual regard for growing plants.

The country homestead has the privacy of ample space, but often suffers from too much open land that reduces the garden to a tiny patch pressed in on all sides by the weight of pasture, field and woodlot. The grounds can be improved immeasurably by breaking some of the space around the house into gardens, grottoes and terraces. Utilitarian rural fences, from sturdy livestock enclosures or driveway snow fencing, to well-built dog runs, can be handsome as well as functional. The white picket fence enclosing the small town and country vegetable or flower garden has an old-fashioned charm, and is not only a delight to the eye, but also keeps animal pests out of the beds and breaks the chilling wind.

Before you buy materials and start setting posts, give some thought to your neighbors. If the backside of your proposed fence is homely or rough, or if the fence cuts off light and air to your neighbor's garden or yard, be prepared for justified complaints. It's common good sense to talk over your fencing plans with the neighbors first—they may want the fence as badly as you do, and may even be willing to share the cost and labor in order to remove the sight of *your* backyard carryings-on from their view. However, they may not envision a fence in the same style or height as you do, and it's far better to find out their preferences before you build it than afterward. A "good neighbor" fence is one that has front and back of equal aesthetic value.

Livestock Fences

Pigs root and dig under fences, horses and cows lean and scratch against them, chickens fly over them and goats take any fence under ten feet high as a personal challenge. All livestock fencing should be built with strength beyond your expectation of its stresses.

The Electric Fence

This is a delightful fence story from B. A. Botkin's *A Treasury of New England Folklore: Stories, Ballads, and Traditions of Yankee Folk.* Mr. Botkin reports:

My friend Al Wilcox of Weston said that he was once driving along a country road in Vermont and had to stop for a few minutes because an old couple were getting a bunch of cattle back into a pasture from which they had strayed out into the road. There was an electric fence across the barway, but they were driving the cattle right over the fence anyhow. When they finally got the cattle all through and signaled to him to come along, he did so, but he stopped and said, "Well, I see you're having quite a lot of trouble with your cattle." And the old lady said, "Wal, you know, the electricity you get nowadays ain't no good."

A poultry yard need not be enclosed with ugly chicken wire, though, admittedly, such wire fencing is easy to put up, contains the hens, admits plenty of light and air, and is fairly inexpensive. A tall picket fence or grapestake fence works just as well, and is handsome, though the original cost is fairly high. The advantage of these semi-solid fences is that they offer a bit of shade in the summer heat. The chicken-wire-fenced yard without shade trees is a baked, sizzling plain in July and August, offering neither comfort nor relief to the panting hens in their downy suits. If you construct a poultry yard with movable fence sections, you gain the advantage of being able to change the contours of the hen run to keep greenery under their feet all summer.

Barbed wire and electric fencing have taken over the world for enclosing large stock inexpensively and with fairly low maintenance. But there is no fixed law that says you must fence with wire. If you like log, split rail or board fences, and can afford the materials or have the raw trees for such fencing growing in your woodlot, they will do the job and blend harmoniously into the landscape. Long after barbed wire strands are sagging and trailing on the ground, a well-made post-and-rail fence will stand. Walter Needham, remembering the way things used to go in *A Book of Country Things,* remarked:

In general I think the old rail fence was the longest-lived one of all. John Gale, the man I learned most from next to Gramp, had a manure shed just beyond his house, and back of that shed until about a year ago was a few sections of rail fence. . . . John Gale's grandfather built that fence over a hundred and twenty-five years ago.

Boundary Fences

The cost of boundary fencing can sometimes be shared by neighbors who plan together and work together. This kind of fencing need not be as elaborate or sturdy as stock fencing, unless one of you keeps animals. Look for a local supply of fencing material—long runs of fence can be very expensive.

Windbreak Fences

Windbreak fencing can vary from living fences of hybrid poplar and evergreens to the familiar lath snow fence. There's a trick to windbreak fences. If you want to build a breeze-cutting fence for patio or garden, don't choose a solid board structure, for the down-drafts and gusts of wind that drop over the top of the fence from a few feet beyond can be more annoying than no fence at all. A rule of thumb for windbreak fencing is to keep to about 50 percent permeability—just enough to break the wind's force without deflecting it radically.

CHAPTER 2

FENCE POSTS

The secret of good fencing lies in the fence posts; they must be sturdy, decay resistant, plumb and in a straight line. They have to be carefully seated to cope with frost heaves or surface stresses. Gate posts must be even stronger and more deeply set to endure the constant flex and torsions of a much-opened gate. Good posts, set properly, will make a long-lived fence. Untreated posts of low decay resistance will last only about *one year* in a humid climate.

Wood decay is the great enemy of fence posts, especially at ground level where the microscopic fungi that feed on wood find the moisture and oxygen they need to grow. The humid Gulf Coast states, in particular, have problems with rotting fence posts. Where termites are found, wood fences are likely to be attacked underground. One study showed that an untreated poplar post that would last only 1.4 years in Mississippi's climate, could endure 14 years in Arizona's dry air.

Choosing the Right Wood

Some woods are more durable than others. In decay-resistant woods, the heartwood—the dark-colored core of the tree—contains chemicals that defy fungi and termites. The sapwood, or outer layers of wood around the core, is not particularly decay resistant. Woodlot owners should know that second-growth trees of decay-resistant wood will have a larger proportion of sapwood to heartwood than first-growth trees, and will have less resistance to decay than the earlier generation. Old slow-growing bald cypress, for example, is extremely resistant to decay, but second-growth bald cypress—even the heartwood—must be treated with preservatives. Untreated pine posts—only moderately resistant to decay—will last barely 3 years in the humid South, up to 6 years in the Northeast, and a good 12 years in the dry West. The same posts, pressure treated, will last 30 to 40 years anywhere. Untreated square redwood posts will last 4 to 24 years, depending on the climate. Western red cedar posts will go 8 to 24 years, and northern white cedar posts will give you 13 to 27 years of sturdy use without preservatives!

Wood Preservatives

Wood preservatives come in two general classes: oil compounds and waterborne salts in solution. Both involve getting the preservative substance, which is destructive to decay-causing fungi and termites, deep into the pores of the wood.

Oil Preservatives Creosote and pentachlorophenol are two commonly used oil preservatives. Creosote is a black or brownish oil made by distilling coal tar, is toxic to the organisms that decay wood, and is a cheap, ef-

11

Native Trees with Decay-Resistant Heartwood

Very Resistant

Black Locust (Robinia pseudoacacia) A very heavy, very hard, strong, stiff wood with good durability and excellent resistance to decay, the Black Locust makes superior fence posts. Its range is restricted to a few Appalachian states.

Red Mulberry (Morus rubra) The Red Mulberry is an eastern tree that grows from southern Vermont to Texas in fertile soils.

Osage Orange (Maclura pomifera) The Osage Orange is extremely strong, heavy, hard and flexible. Although it has a small range in the Southern Plain states and the Midwest, it is used there for long-lasting fence posts.

Resistant

Catalpa (Catalpa bignonioides) The Catalpa is a quick-growing tree unfortunately prey to frost damage and insects. It goes down easily in storms. The Catalpa was once widely planted for fence posts.

Eastern Red Cedar (Juniperus virginiana) The most widely distributed tree-sized conifer in the eastern United States, the Eastern Red Cedar grows from Maine to the Rockies. Although very resistant to decay, and once widely used for fence posts, it has become expensive and is more often made into cedar chests, closets, pencils and tourist novelties. Fence post buyers have to content themselves with other cedar posts. *Caution*: The red cedar is host to a fungus, the cedar-apple rust, which can affect apple trees not resistant to this affliction growing nearby. Keep red cedar posts away from apple trees or grow cultivars that are resistant to cedar-apple rust, such as Nova Easygro and Liberty.

Black Cherry (Prunus serotina) A widely distributed tree, the Black Cherry grows from Nova Scotia to North Dakota and from Florida to Arizona. Its hard, dense wood is much valued for furniture making. It is generally too valuable to use for fence posts, but if you have post-sized black cherry trees growing on your property, you may want to thin some out for posts.

American Chestnut (Castanea dentata) Frequently used as yesterday's fence posts and rails, this tree was known as "the farmer's friend," for it was a rapid grower with durable and rot-resistant wood, was easy to work and to split, and propagated lustily. From the Appalachians to southern Maine thousands of miles of chestnut fencing snaked across the countryside. When the blight began killing off our chestnuts in 1904, the prime material for fence posts and rails went too. Today you may occasionally find dead chestnut stumpwood still standing. It may yet be usable for posts or rails. If you find a large dead chestnut with sound wood, your nearest cabinet-maker will prize the wood for constructing furniture.

Post Oak (Quercus stellata) The heavy, close-grained wood of the Post Oak is durable and long lasting in contact with the soil, and is widely used for fence posts. It grows in a range from the Middle Atlantic to the southern states. Other oaks used for posts are the Bur Oak, Gambel Oak, Oregon White Oak and White Oak. Avoid both the Red Oak and Black Oak (*Quercus rubra* and *Quercus velutina*) for posts as they have little or no resistance to decay.

Redwood (Sequoia sempervirens) The large and magnificent Redwood grows along the northern Pacific coast where the climate is damp and foggy. Its heartwood is highly decay resistant, but the reputation of Redwood as the outstanding long-lasting wood is somewhat overrated. Osage Orange, Red Mulberry and Black Locust are more decay resistant in their heartwood. Many dealers sell Redwood sapwood as decay resistant, though the sapwood is only moderately able to withstand the assaults of fungi and dampness.

There are several other tree species of considerable decay resistance, but because they grow in restricted habitats or because their wood is prized for other uses, they are not generally recognized as post timber. These include the Black Walnut, Pacific Yew, Arizona Cypress and Sassafras.

Moderately Resistant

Bald Cypress (Taxodium distichum) Found in the coastal South, the Bald Cypress has wood that is heavy, hard and strong. The heartwood of the old first-growth trees was outstanding in its resistance to decay, so much so that it was used for river pilings, but the sapwood decays quite easily. Since the second-growth Bald Cypress, containing a large proportion of sapwood, is about all we have today, Bald Cypress has lost much of its reputation of old.

Honey Locust (Gleditsia triacanthos) Common from the Mississippi Valley eastward, the wood of the Honey Locust is heavy and durable; it is used for fence posts and railroad ties.

Eastern White Pine (Pinus strobus) Not much heartwood of the Eastern White Pine is available as most of the timber taken is second growth.

Longleaf Pine (Pinus australis) The Longleaf Pine is the turpentine pine of the South, and a valuable timber tree. Only limited amounts of heartwood are available since most of the timber harvested now is second growth.

Tamarack (Larix laricina) The Larch or Tamarack grows from Maine to Lake Superior, one of the widest-ranging conifers we have. The wood is heavy, hard and decay resistant. It makes quite good fence posts.

Other trees whose heartwood is moderately resistant to decay include the Douglas Fir, Western Larch, Swamp Chestnut Oak and Slash Pine.

Very Little Resistance

The wood of these trees is susceptible to decay and will not last long unless treated with preservatives or used in a dry climate.

Alder	Hickory
Ash	Magnolia
Aspen	Maple
Basswood	Red and Black Oak
Beech	Pine (except those
Birch	listed above)
Buckeye	Poplar
Butternut	Spruce
Cottonwood	Sweetgum
Elm	Sycamore
Hackberry	Willow
Hemlock	

SOURCE: University of Wisconsin Extension Service Publication A2982, "Preservative Treatment of Wood for Farm Use," by Rodney C. DeGroot and Bruce R. Johnson, p. 3.

fective wood preservative in use for a long time. But creosote-treated wood cannot be painted, has a powerful odor, and gives off vapors above ground that are toxic to growing plants, and will kill plants whose root systems come near the tainted posts underground. Creosoted posts have no place in the garden.

Pentachlorophenol in heavy oils is used in commercial pressure treatments of lumber and posts, and has as good a track record in preventing decay as creosote, but the wood is not paintable after treatment, and is *poisonous to plants*. Again, the odor is heavy and disagreeable, and the vapor toxic to plants.

Waterborne Preservatives Preservatives of this type usually leave the wood clean to the touch, paintable and relatively odorless. There are no toxic vapors to burn the leaves of nearby plants, but many gardeners claim underground root systems of plants do not flourish when planted near salts-treated posts. The most common treatments are Chromated Copper Arsenate (CCA) and Ammoniacal Copper Arsenate (ACA), but there are others.

Treated posts usually have the preservative substance forced into the wood under pressure, and will last up to 50 years in the ground. They are excellent for boundaries, stock fences and such, but, for your garden, make every effort to use natural decay-resistant heartwood posts. There's not much point in protecting your plants from invading goats and deer if you're going to poison the earth with toxic fence posts. If you buy posts, look on the butt ends for ratings. The American Wood Preservers Bureau rates posts treated for below-ground use as LP-22. Fencing material to be used above ground gets a mark of LP-2.

Posts from the Woodlot

If you have a supply of decay-resistant trees growing in your woodlot you can cut your own fence posts. You can add to the lives of your posts by soaking them in chemical or oil solutions for a few days. Old barrels make good dip tanks, for only the bottom section of the post— the part that goes below ground—need be treated.

A very big problem with treating your own fence posts is what to do with the leftover oil or solution. Environmental protection laws prohibit the casual dumping habits of yesteryear.

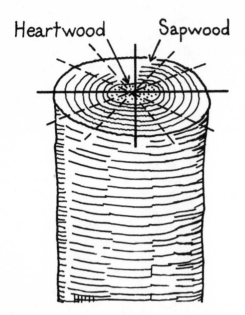

Heartwood   Sapwood

The hard, tough heartwood of a tree is strongly compressed dead tissue, squeezed tight by the growing sapwood. Heartwood is more decay resistant and longer lasting than sapwood. Every fence post should contain some heartwood. Traditionally, logs are split into twelfths, as shown, to make 12 fence posts, each with a bit of heartwood.

Every state has different rules, so before you undertake the job, contact your state Department of Environmental Protection and find out how to get rid of the toxic leftovers.

Fence posts are usually cut in winter or spring, and are used green in the Northeast. The posts must have the bark peeled off to prevent decay. Green posts take a preservative dip better than seasoned posts.

If you cut large trees for posts, remember that a good fence post must contain some of the heartwood of the tree. There's no problem if you are using the whole trunks of small post-sized trees, but splitting a big fellow into posts has to be done right. The familiar triangular fence posts that mark thousands of farm fields have been split into twelfths in the old traditional manner that gives some heartwood to every post.

You need a maul, wedges and a saw to make fence posts.

1. Pre-cut the log to proper fence post lengths.
2. Snap a chalk line the length of the log, and, driving in the wedges along the line, split the log in half lengthwise.

3. Quarter the log, then split each quarter into thirds if the diameter of the tree allows it.

Post Sizes

A heavy fence 4 feet high should have 4 x 4 posts, and corner posts and gate posts should be even stouter—6 x 6 or 8 x 8. Posts commonly can be bought in 6-, 7- and 8-foot lengths so that they can be set 2 feet or more into the ground. Posts should be set no more than 8 feet apart; if there is going to be stress on the fence, they should be set closer. As a rule of thumb, posts are set 2 feet into the earth, but corner and gate posts should be set 3 feet deep or one-third of the post's total length. So, a 4-foot fence would call for 6-foot on-line posts and seven-footers for the end posts.

There are situations when the posts should be set especially deep—when the fence is to be higher than 6 feet, when the horizontal boarding will be very heavy, when large animals are to be held in by the fence, when strong prevailing winds beat constantly against the fence, or when the soil is light and sandy. If you live in a frost-free region, set stressed fence posts in concrete. If you live where frost heaving is a problem, set posts instead in tamped soil, gravel and rock; these materials will rise and fall with the frosts, whereas a concrete plug may be permanently tilted out of line by frost action.

If the posts are to be mortised (cut with holes to receive rails) or dadoed (cut with notches to accept boards), this work should be done *before* the posts are set. The holes have to be perfectly aligned to accommodate the fence siding or rails, lest the fence refuse to line up properly and boards pop off.

Marking the Spot

Although you may have a clear vision of where the fence will go on a piece of ground, don't be tempted to set posts by eye—you'll end up with a wavering, crooked structure. There's more to a straight fence than looks: the straighter the line, the more stable the fence.

1. Lay out a straight fence line by driving in stakes at each end of the proposed line, then running mason's twine—a tightly twisted cord that resists stretching—between the stakes. You will need support stakes every 50 feet or so to keep the twine from sagging.

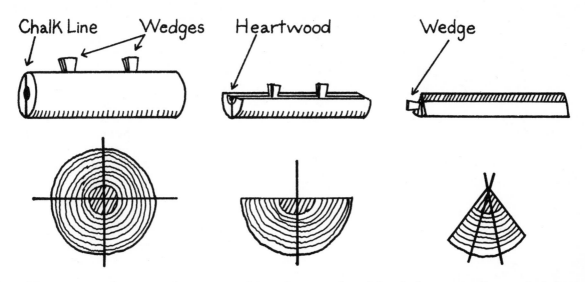

Chalk Line   Wedges   Heartwood   Wedge

In making your own fence posts, logs are sawed into the correct length for the fence posts, then marked down their length with a clean, straight chalk line. The logs are split in half by driving wedges into the log along the chalk line. The same steps are repeated to quarter the log or to make even smaller sub-divisions if the log is of good size. The beginning fence post maker will soon develop a feel for this work.

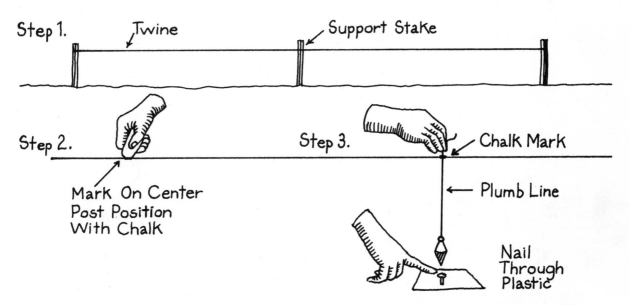

Step 1.   Twine   Support Stake

Step 2.   Mark On Center Post Position With Chalk

Step 3.   Chalk Mark   Plumb Line   Nail Through Plastic

A carefully laid out fence repays its builder with beauty and endurance. The twine marking the fence line must be kept taut with a support stake every 50 feet or less. The post positions are marked on the line with chalk. A plumb bob helps you transfer the chalk mark position on the line to the ground with accuracy and precision. A helper to tag the ground position of the post with a roofing nail through a scrap of bright plastic makes the job easy and companionable.

2. On the taut twine mark the correct *on center* position for each post with colored chalk.

3. Use a plumb-bob and line held against the chalk mark to get the exact position for the post onto the ground. Don't try to do it by eye unless you want odd spaces between the posts with the inevitable short boards or overlong rails. Mark the position for each post on the ground with a large common nail pierced through a scrap of plastic marking tape or paper. The plastic tape used by surveyors and lumbermen has the advantage of staying visible for months in case your fence project gets interrupted.

Post Holes

There are three good tools for digging post holes, and the shovel is *not* one of them. Shovels and spades make wide, sloppy, unstable holes that allow the post to wobble and lean. The proper tools are the post hole digger, also called a clamshell in some regions, and best used on medium-hard soils; the hand auger for soft soils; and the gasoline-powered drill for big jobs on very hard soil. The two-person power drill is reputedly safer to use. All of these tools can be rented from equipment rental businesses, fencing dealers, farm supply stores and sometimes local rural hardware stores. Post hole diggers and hand augers frequently turn up at farm auctions for a few dollars. Suppliers of new post and fence tools are listed in the mail-order sources box in the Appendices.

A length of 2 x 4 makes a good soil tamper, used when you fill in the hole around the post.

If you have quite a few posts to set, it's worth the trouble to round off the top of the 2 x 4 so that it fits the hands comfortably.

Setting the Posts

1. Dig the holes at least 4 to 6 inches deeper than the post's required depth for drainage. The bottom should be as level as you can get it.

2. Set a flat base stone in the bottom of the hole so that the end grain of the post is not in direct contact with the soil.

3. Stand the post in place and fill in around it with 6 inches of gravel or small stones and tamp them down vigorously with a length of 2 x 4.

4. Fill in the hole with the excavated soil and some gravel mixed in for drainage a few inches at a time, tamping thoroughly. Correct

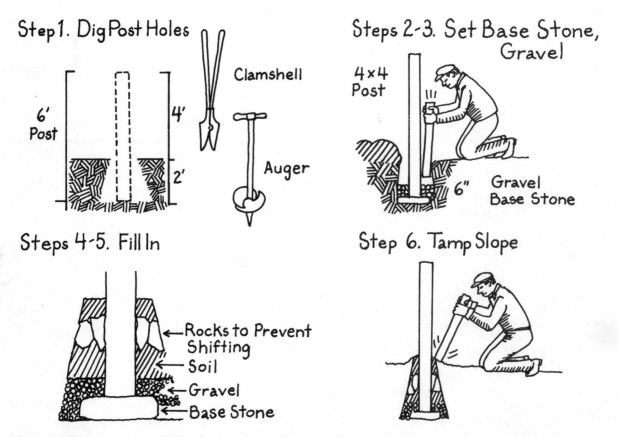

The straggling, rag-tag-and-bobtail fences that outline the fields and pastures of many old farms are built on posts that were simply pounded into the earth. Inevitably these pitch and lean. But a properly set line of posts will stand straight and undeviating for generations. Above is the correct way to set a post.

the alignment of the post as you go, using a level to be sure it is plumb.

5. Near the ground surface, jam several rocks into the hole to keep the post from shifting.

6. Build a tamped earth slope up above ground surface so that the rain will run off away from the post.

Concrete-Set Posts

Fence posts that will suffer stress in frost-free areas or where the soil is loose and sandy should be set in concrete. Dig the hole and set the post as outlined in steps 1 to 3 for post setting, but then fill the hole with concrete. Keep the anchorage at least 6 inches below ground level, and fill up the hole with tamped earth after the concrete has set for several days. Concrete is porous and will trap and hold water right around the post if it is built up right to the surface. The concrete mix should be 2 parts cement, 3 parts sand and 5 parts gravel, with water added sparingly so that the mixture is on the stiff side. Let the posts stand undisturbed for several days before adding rails or boards.

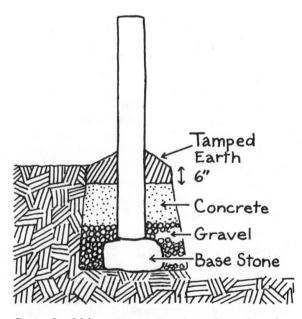

Posts should be set in concrete in regions of sandy soil, or where frost heaving is not a problem. The procedure is similar for setting posts in earth, but the fill is concrete. Notice the sloped, tamped earth mound above the soil line for good run-off of rain water.

Driven Posts

In the old days, if the fence was to run over good soil where not too many stones lay, posts were driven directly into the ground without digging a hole. This was a two-person job: one held the post steady and plumb, and the other, perhaps standing on the back of a wagon to get a better swing, drove the post into the earth with a special maul. The huge maul head was slightly hollowed on the striking face, and was often made of elm, for elm, with its twisted cross-grain, resisted splitting. It was more likely that the post would split, especially if it were chestnut, under the blows of the maul. Shaping the posts by cutting off their corners lessened the chances of a split post.

Frost-heaved posts had to be driven in again each spring, and split posts were a common casualty unless a scantling board was laid on the post for the maul to strike against.

Aligning the Posts

Lining up and setting posts is a two-person job—one person to hold and realign the post, the other to hold up the level and fill in the hole around the post. (See illustration on page 18.)

1. To get the posts perfectly aligned in a short fence—about 50 feet—first set the two end posts, taking great care to get them parallel and plumb.

2. Cut three 1 by 2 by 2-inch spacer blocks from a scrap 1 x 2, and tack them onto the end posts at the same height, about a foot up from ground level. Stretch a length of mason's twine between these two spacers, from post to post. It should be taut and level.

3. Set in the posts along the line with the taut twine as a guide, holding up the third spacer block between the twine and the post for perfect alignment. If you have a good eye you can line up the posts without the spacer.

4. Remember to use the level to get the posts perpendicular to the ground in both directions.

Long country fences that stretch away into the distance obviously cannot have their end posts linked by tight mason's twine. Work a long fence in 50-foot sections.

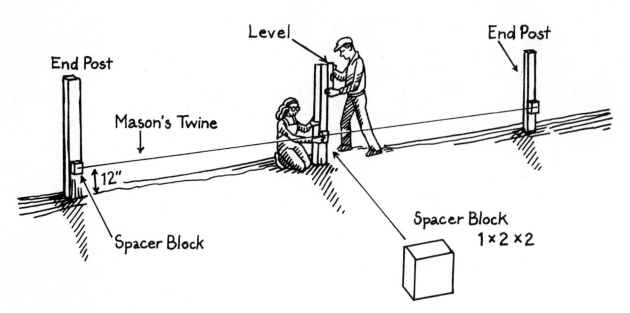

Aligning posts and setting them in the ground is a two-person job that is not difficult but is exacting. Remember to check the position of the post both on a north-south and an east-west line with the level so it is perpendicular from all sides.

Leveling the Posts

Many board fence designs, such as rails set into mortised or dadoed posts, or capped fences, demand posts all of the same height. On level ground it's not too difficult to get the tops of the posts level too.

1. Set the first post at the correct alignment and height.

2. Drive a nail partway into the center top of this "perfect" post, then tie onto the nail enough of that indispensable mason's twine to reach to the end post in the fence line, or to a post 50 feet or less away.

3. Set the far end post loosely in place and tap a nail into its center top, then tie the twine to the nail. The twine should be drawn taut.

4. Jockey the far end post up and down, using a line level to determine when the twine is level. Then seat the post at the correct height.

5. Fill in firmly around the post, rechecking alignment, plumb and levelness with the original post. Let the taut, level twine serve as the guide for leveling the tops of the posts in between.

Another Way If you are tired of twine or short of it for leveling and aligning, there is a simpler way to set posts level. Use an *unwarped* 2 x 4 long enough to extend a little beyond any two posts—that is, if your posts are set 6 feet apart on center, use a 7- or 8-foot length of 2 x 4, but be *sure* it's not warped. (It may take you quite a while to find this elusive object at your friendly neighborhood lumberyard.) Set the first post plumb, level and in line, simply lay the 2 x 4 across it and the next loosely set post, place the level on the 2 x 4 and fiddle with the loose post until you get it level and plumb, then fill in the hole solidly and go on to the next post with your trusty 2 x 4.

Uneven Terrain

If you are running a fence across sloping ground you have a choice of two approaches: you can run the fence parallel with the slope—a method called "contour fencing," or you can build short sections that drop like a set of stairs—"step fencing." To my eye, contour fencing always looks rather strange, as though the fence were rushing downhill into a hole in the ground,

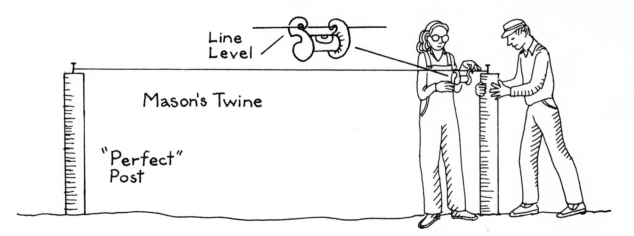

The "perfect" post is not only nicely aligned perpendicularly, but is also level with its companion posts. A line level makes the task much easier. Long fences should be aligned and leveled in short sections.

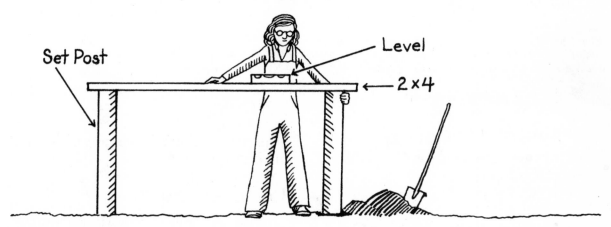

An upwarped 2 × 4 long enough to span the distance between two posts and an ordinary carpenter's level provide an alternate way to level fence post tops.

like a tape measure disappearing into its case—but if you like contour fencing, by all means build it.

Setting the posts of contour fencing with a level and a 2 x 4 simply doesn't work; the mason's twine is essential. Step fencing involves a somewhat different approach, and you have to know the slope measurement.

Step Fencing

1. Set stakes at the beginning and end of the fence line.
2. Attach the indispensable mason's twine at the ground level of the uphill stake.

3. Tie the twine tautly to the downhill stake, making sure the line is level. Use the level rather than trust your eye.
4. Measure the distance between the ground and the level twine at the downhill stake—this measurement is the *slope height*.

$$\frac{\text{slope height}}{\text{number of sections}} = \frac{\text{the amount of}}{\text{drop for each section}}$$

For example, you plan to set your posts 6 feet apart. In 24 feet of fence you will have four sections. In the illustration on page 20 the slope

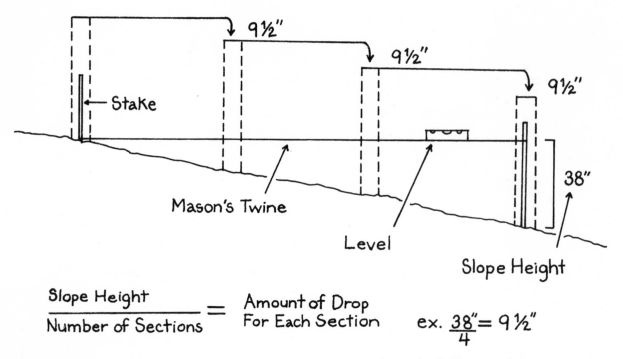

$$\frac{\text{Slope Height}}{\text{Number of Sections}} = \frac{\text{Amount of Drop}}{\text{For Each Section}} \qquad \text{ex. } \frac{38''}{4} = 9\tfrac{1}{2}''$$

Step fencing is a neat and tidy way to deal with a fence line across sloping land. This procedure averages out the drop of the slope into even steps. Though the example given here has a drop of 9½ inches between posts, the measurement depends on the slope of your land. Such a fence is custom-tailored to your terrain.

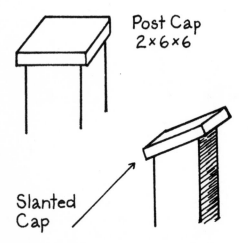

A post cap is simply a small, overhanging rooflet to protect the fence post from rain, ice and snow seeping down into the end grain. A capped post will last longer than a bare-headed post.

height is 38 inches. Divide the slope height by the number of sections:

$$\frac{38}{4} = 9\tfrac{1}{2}$$

This means that the top of each post must be 9½ inches lower than the post uphill from it,

giving the finished fence the appearance of regularly graduated steps.

Repairing Posts

Posts are the first part of a fence to go. They will last longer if they are capped with a section of board. Sometimes one sees posts with slanted tops and caps; these miniature shanty roofs help the rain run off quickly.

If you have an old fence with some posts wobbling and leaning because they're rotted underground, you can restore the fence's strength and usefulness by adding a new post support. It's usual for the aboveground section of an old fence to be sound, with good rails and boards still attached to truncated but solid upper posts.

Don't try to detach the boards or dig out the old, rotted, underground mess with the idea of putting in a new post. It's miserable and unnecessary work to dig out the old post, especially if it was set in concrete. Instead, dig a new hole directly beside the old post, then set in a new decay-resistant post brace about 4 or 5 feet long, so that only 2½ feet are above ground. Set in this post brace with the same care you would a new post (see section on setting posts

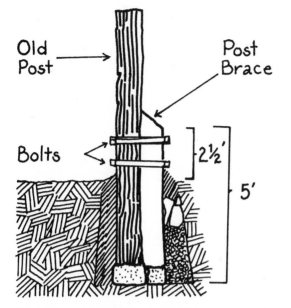

Old Post

Post Brace

Bolts

2½'

5'

Repairing a rotted fence post with a new post brace flush against the old post is the easiest and most effective procedure. Digging out an old post is a long, hard job that is rarely necessary.

earlier in this chapter). The top of the brace should be cut at a 45° angle for rain run-off. When the brace is set solid and firm, snugged up against the sound wood of the old upper post, bolt the brace to the old post where the wood is soundest with two ½-inch-diameter carriage bolts, nuts and washers—*voila!*—a sturdy, up-

right post again. The reason for using only a short brace instead of a full-length post is purely aesthetic; it looks better from a distance, whereas a second post would stand out like—well, like a second post.

If most of the old posts have rotted at their bases and are in poor condition above ground, brace repairs have come too late. You will have to set new posts. But don't make yourself a great deal of unnecessary work by dismantling the fence and laboriously digging up the old posts. Instead, dig new holes and set new posts midway between the old ones exactly on line, then nail the siding, still attached to the old posts, right into the new ones. Leave the old posts alone—if you pull them away from the siding you'll have loose butt ends flapping in the breeze and a very wobbly fence that won't keep anything but buttercups from breaking through it.

If you absolutely must remove an old post, first cut it off at ground level and very carefully remove the nails from the boards. Try to get out the rotted wood, concrete, stones, fill and whatever else is underground without making an immense crater. A crowbar, clamshell or even a trowel will help a little to keep the hole narrow. Finally, set in the new post and nail the boards back on. Don't nail through the old holes. If the siding has become brittle with age, you may first have to drill holes of a slightly smaller diameter than the nails to keep from splitting the wood.

CHAPTER 3

CHOOSING THE RIGHT FENCE

The types of fences to choose from are varied, and the temptation to decide on a fence for reasons of appearance or sentiment is ever present. Resist any impulses that don't take into account the purpose of the fence, the terrain and the neighborhood.

The Old-Fashioned Four-Board Fence

In great-grandfather's day, 7-foot posts and 16-foot boards made this a standard board fence down on the farm. It's still a good fence—sturdy, attractive, simple to make. But now the lumber is expensive unless you have your own sawmill or an independent income—then you can encircle your ranch with miles of this fence.

Four-board fencing is meant to keep livestock in or out of a field. The posts are 4 x 4s, the boards 16-foot 1 x 6s. If the fence was to be "bull-nay"—strong enough to say "nay" to the most furious bull—in the old days, the posts were 6 x 6s and the boards were 2 inches thick.

To make this fence, set the posts 8 feet apart on center. The boards are nailed on so that only two boards butt together on the post, the other two spanning the post to prevent sagging. Stout 10-penny nails or larger are used.

In the past each post was capped, partly to prevent rain water from trickling down the post and along the nails, which were not galvanized in the old days and tended to rust in a few years.

Alternate Post Board Fence This variation makes a stronger fence. To construct this fence, lay out the fence line as usual with taut mason's twine, but set each post ½ inch away from the twine on alternate sides of the line. Setting the posts in this manner leaves enough space for the 1-inch board siding which is nailed to the posts on alternate sides. An alternate post board fence is very firm and stable.

Braced-Board Fence Even stronger than the alternate board fence is the braced fence. The farmer can get away with narrower boards here because of the extra strength in the design.

Horse Enclosures Corrals and horse fences have some extra touches. Modern corrals are 5- to 6-foot-high post-and-board fences that take heavy 6 x 6 posts and 16-foot 2 x 6 boards. The posts are set no more than 8 feet apart. Braced boards are never used in a horse corral because of the possible danger of a horse getting a foot wedged into the acute angle. The boards are always attached on the inside of a horse enclosure so that the animals won't bump into protruding posts, and the fence surface presented to them has as few indentations as possible. Often the corners in square or rectangular cor-

23

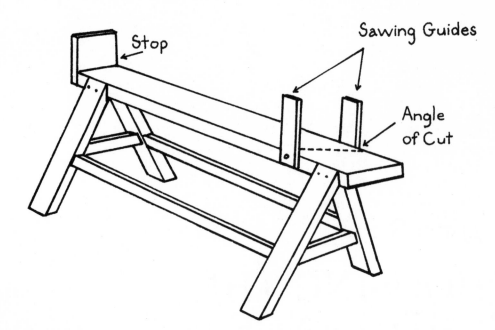

Stop

Sawing Guides

Angle
of Cut

A picket bench makes the tedious job of hand-sawing pickets faster and more precise. You can modify a sturdy sawhorse into a temporary picket bench, or build one from scrap lumber whose sole reason to exist is to lighten the burden of the picket cutter.

rals are closed off so that some luckless horse cannot be backed or maneuvered into a corner by more aggressive comrades.

Kickboards When animals that dig or squeeze under fences are a problem, a kickboard run along the bottom of the posts, close to but not touching the soil, does the trick.

The Picket Fence

The neat colonial picket fence around the vegetable garden, the ornamental Victorian picket fence with its notches and scrollwork setting off the house and rose garden, the tall picket fence surrounding the old-fashioned poultry yard—all gave grace and airy lightness to home, sweet home, in the past. Picket fences still make side streets in many small towns attractive and beguiling, but, sadly, today's Saturday handyman seems to eschew the lacy picket in favor of a low, sketchy, two-rail structure that is not so much a fence as a wooden line drawn across the front of his property. When a new picket fence does go up, it is apt to be a plain picket of wider boards than yesteryear, creating a somewhat monotonous effect rather than delighting the eye. Yet probably no other

fence design offers such a range of creative design possibilities to the homeowner as the picket.

Cutting pickets is one of those tasks you do outdoors on a nice day until you get tired of it, or in the home workshop or barn on a rainy afternoon when nothing else is pressing you for time. It can be tedious work. Now we use C-clamps and sabre saws to cut pickets, but it used to be done with a hand saw and a "picket bench." The picket bench was a narrow little sawhorse with a stop at one end to butt the pickets against, and two scraps of wood nailed to the front edges to give the correct cutting angle for the picket points. If you're cutting your own pickets you might want to take a few minutes to make a picket bench—the job becomes easier.

The average picket fence is 3 to 4 feet high. All the pickets should be cut ahead of time. If you shrink from the thought of cutting hundreds or even thousands of pickets yourself, you can take the 1 x 3s to a woodworking shop to have the special pattern custom cut. Fence dealers and lumberyards rarely carry anything more interesting than plain old pickets. But if you are going to the expense and trouble of making a picket fence, you might as well have it as satisfyingly intricate as you like.

Constructing the Basic Picket Fence

For a picket fence 3 to 4 feet high, build in 6-foot sections. The standard picket is 3 inches wide, and the space between pickets should be a little narrower than the pickets themselves, about 2½ inches. This means that 100 feet of fence will take about 216 3-inch pickets. You can, of course, vary the proportions and sizes to suit your taste. The narrower the pickets, the more fragile and airy the fence will appear. (See illustration on page 26.)

1. Lay out the main fence line with the mason's twine and stakes, then set 4 x 4 squared posts every 6 feet on center. The posts may be topped with elaborate caps or knobs or carved pineapples if you like. The posts should be dadoed (pierced with rectangular grooves cut to size) first to receive the rails that back the pickets.

2. Set the top and bottom rails into the dadoed posts, or you may wish to run the top rail as a cap over the top of the posts. The top rail should be at least 6 inches below the level of the picket points. Lengths of 2 x 4s make sturdy rails. Use a carpenter's framing square to get the rails at right angles to the upright posts, and take the greatest care to be positive they are level, or the pickets may line up out of true, like endless falling dominoes.

3. Use galvanized nails (box nails are less likely to split the pickets than common nails) to nail the pickets to the rails. Be absolutely sure that the first picket is straight up and down—vertically plumb—by using a level. Some people like to measure carefully along the rail and make marks where the pickets are to go before they embark on an orgy of nailing, but a better way is to make a picket spacer of the desired width and the same height as the pickets. The spacer must be straight and true. At the top of the picket spacer nail a little cleat at right angles to its sides. This lets you hang the spacer on the top rail, slap a picket into its correct position beside the spacer, nail the picket

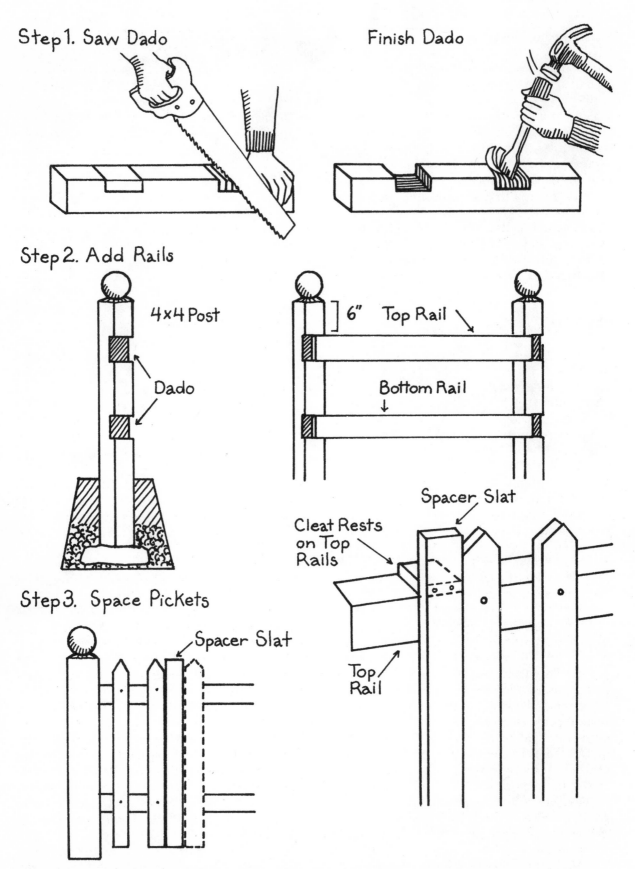

Step 1. Saw Dado

Finish Dado

Step 2. Add Rails

4 x 4 Post

Dado

6"   Top Rail

Bottom Rail

Spacer Slat

Cleat Rests
on Top
Rails

Top
Rail

Step 3. Space Pickets

Spacer Slat

The most careful work in constructing a picket fence goes for nothing if the first picket is out of line. Double-check all horizontal and vertical alignments.

firmly home, move the spacer over to the far side of the fresh-nailed picket, slap another picket into place, and so on until the final picket is nailed smartly onto the rails.

As you work along the fence, check the pickets' vertical alignment every now and then. If that little cleat at the top of the spacer is not exactly at right angles, or works loose as you use it, all the pickets may exhibit a rakish, leaning posture that will certainly make your fence draw the eyes of passersby.

Colonial picket fences had a rather menacing air; they were wider than usual, about 4 inches, and sawed at one diagonal angle so that nailed in place they had the look of jagged teeth.

The Wattle Hurdle

Hurdles are a very old kind of lightweight, movable fence. In medieval England they were made by hurdle makers who lived for weeks in small huts near the source of their raw materials—ash, hazel and willow. When American pioneers rolled onto the treeless plains of the West, they were hard pressed for fencing materials, and a local type of fencing similar to the wattle hurdle was used. Banks of earth several feet high were thrown up, and stakes 6 to 8 feet tall were driven into these ramparts. Willow branches from the trees that grow along watercourses were woven in between the stakes as rough, untrimmed weaving rods. These bristling fences with twigs sticking out in all directions lasted as long as 15 years with annual repairs.

Although the art of hurdle making is now almost unknown in this country, hurdles are easy to make and have a hundred uses for gardeners. They can be propped up to make a cool and shady roof for lettuces and spinach when the summer days get hot and laggy; they make instant portable screens for patio and lawn, or wherever a patch of shade is wanted. They are quickly built windbreaks for spring luncheons *al fresco,* or for tender tall-stalked flowers such as delphiniums which suffer in wind. Several of them joined together can make a temporary poultry enclosure. They can also be used in the garden as handsome supports for climbing peas or cucumbers.

Making hurdles is a pleasant springtime job that anyone reasonably handy with a supply of flexible "weavers" can do, but to make them properly with twisted-end hazel rods and a central gap—the twilly hole—for carrying one or a dozen hurdles, takes skill. Advanced hurdle makers keep the cut ends and split sides to the back of the hurdle for a smoother appearance, even as basket makers keep them to the inside. In a sense, a hurdle is nothing more than a huge flat, basket-woven screen.

Making the Hurdle

To make a hurdle you need the following:

Mold This is a stout 2 x 8 plank 8 feet long, or a log of the same length, bored every 8 or 10 inches with a 1-inch-diameter hole. The mold must be pegged down securely before you start to work. A wobbling mold means loose, sloppy weaving.

Sails The uprights, or sails, are straight young saplings peeled of their bark, each about 4 feet high. These sails form the supports of the hurdle and are set into the holes in the mold. The two end sails should be stouter than the others for extra strength.

Weaving Rods Traditionally, long, thin hazel rods are trimmed and then split lengthwise with a very sharp billhook, the English farmer's most handy tool. Weavers are gathered and worked in the spring and early summer while the hazel is most flexible. You can use willow or osier or any other slim, flexible shrub or branch that grows in your region. You need not peel the weavers. (See illustration on page 28.)

1. Set up the mold, pegging it securely to the ground.
2. Cut and peel the sails and set them in place in the mold. Use saplings, not branch wood. Softwood is not recommended. Maple, ash, hickory, oak, osage orange or the saplings of any fence post timber material all make good sails. If you use sails that are not decay resistant, take care not to let the finished hurdle stand on the soil.
3. Prepare the weaving rods. Red osier makes a fine and beautiful screen if you choose the longest whips. By cutting back a stand of wild osier one year, you will get a fine growth of straight, branchless whips the next spring that are excellent both for basket weaving and hurdle weaving.
4. Weave in the rods, using the heaviest ones near the base of the hurdle. At each end, take care to twist the weaver or it will break when it dries. Keep the cut ends and the split

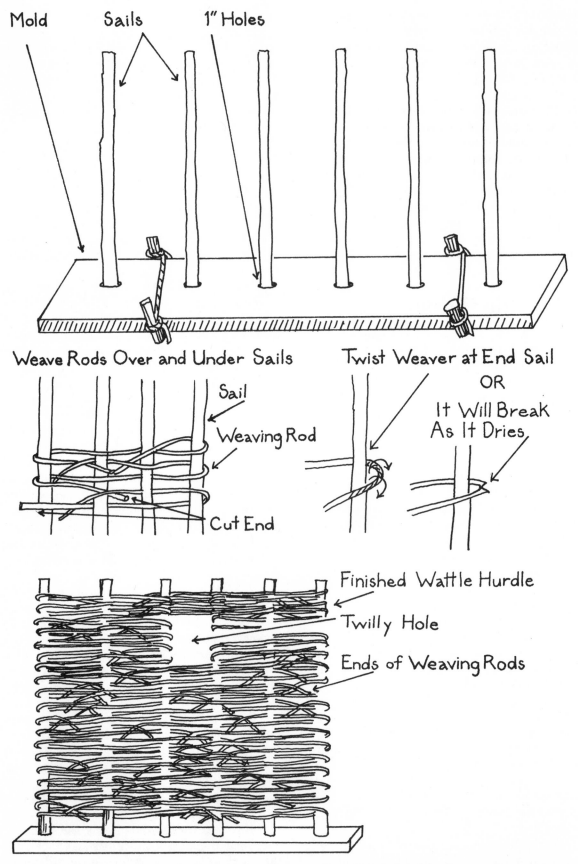

Mold   Sails   1" Holes

Weave Rods Over and Under Sails

Sail

Weaving Rod

Cut End

Twist Weaver at End Sail

OR

It Will Break As It Dries

Finished Wattle Hurdle

Twilly Hole

Ends of Weaving Rods

The medieval woven wattle hurdle has many modern uses. Beautiful, lightweight fence sections can be woven with natural, indigenous materials from your area such as willow, osier, twisted rushes or split saplings.

sides (if you use split weavers) all on the back for a smoother, more attractive hurdle. Pack the weaving tight every so often with a stout beater stick. Work the weaving until you are about 3 feet up the sails, or roughly two-thirds of the total height.

5. Here the twilly hole is worked in. (If you don't want a twilly hole, keep weaving until you get the desired height.) Simply twist the weaver rods back on each other to leave a gap between the two center sails. The upper edge of the twilly hole can be strengthened by weaving in five or six extra small rods. When the twilly hole is big enough to suit you, continue working weavers all the way across the hurdle until the sails are filled with weaving.

The projecting sail ends can be sharpened with an axe and set in the ground with pressure if the sails are of decay-resistant wood. A number of hurdles can be linked together with twine or wire so that they fold like an accordion when carried on a long pole thrust through the twilly holes, and borne on the shoulder.

Other Movable Fences

Movable fences were important in English sheep-raising country during the period of the open field system. By hauling fences around to

Railroad Windbreak

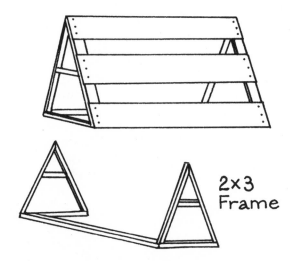

2×3 Frame

The railroad windbreak is a portable, small snow fence that lets you control drifts in short driveways or house entrances, or near the trash cans. Experiment with two or three until you get the correct placement to cause the wind's velocity to be broken and the snow load dumped in a more convenient spot.

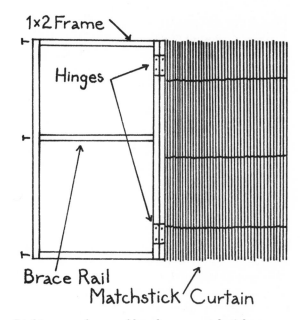

1×2 Frame

Hinges

Brace Rail

Matchstick Curtain

Light screen fences of bamboo or matchstick curtains tacked onto a frame are quickly made and have dozens of uses. They provide quick shade on a porch, or a patch of cool comfort near the dog house. They can be hinged and set up in pairs like a folding screen, or temporarily attached to a porch railing or fence section. Gardeners will find another use for them—as a roof for shade-loving plants such as impatiens.

new locations every day the sheep could be "folded" on different parts of the common-held arable land, and this meant that in time all the crop land got a good sprinkling of manure and a thorough working-over by the sharp cloven hooves of the sheep—the Rototiller of earlier centuries.

For today's gardener a section or two of movable fence is very handy. A picket or lath fence which has one or two portable sections lets you remove those pieces of fence to get machinery in and out of the garden, and even lets you change the shape of the garden to suit crop rotations and green manure cover crop plantings. The old-style "railroad windbreak" portable fence is tremendously useful in preventing snow drifting in the winter driveway, or it lets you arrange the snow so that it heaps over your tender grapevines to insulate them from the bitter winds and bone-cracking freeze of the open air. New yards where shade trees are still too small to cast a comfortable shadow become cool and pleasant with portable panels.

You can make a portable shade fence in a hurry by building two or three light frames with a brace rail out of 1 x 2s, hinging the panels together to make a folding screen and tacking a section of bamboo or matchstick curtain on the face of each section. Keep the panels fairly small for ease in handling. You can buy bamboo curtain from discount stores, Sears or Montgomery Ward, as well as many hardware and home furnishing stores. If the panels are going to stay outdoors in all weather, be sure to use preservative-treated lumber and whole bamboo, not the split kind.

The Solid Board Fence

The solid board fence is a fast way to get outdoor privacy, and the designs for such fences seem endless: horizontal, vertical or diagonal boards, panels of alternating board directions, open tops, textured boards, board-and-batten, tongue-and-groove and so on. Be warned, though, that horizontal boarding looks quite peculiar if the fence is on sloping ground.

These privacy fences are tall—6 to 8 feet high. The construction is not difficult, but the cost of lumber can be formidable. Rough-cut lumber makes a good-looking, natural fence and is much cheaper than fancy-grade finished lumber or expensive redwood or pecky cypress.

A 6-foot-high fence demands 4 x 4 posts set at least 2 feet deep. The end and gate posts must be 6 x 6s or more robust 8 x 8s set 3 feet deep.

Deciding on the design for a privacy fence is the most pleasant stage of the whole process, and it pays to develop a habit of fence-looking on your travels around the countryside. Look closely at neighbors' fences, the fences in public gardens, and, of course, the illustrations in books and magazines. An hour or two at the public library browsing through the glossy California illustrations in garden design and outdoor living books will give you more ideas than you can use in a lifetime. When you look at real fences on highways and byways, keep a sharp eye on fence problems—decay at board joints, leaning posts, scaling paint, broken pickets—and vow not to duplicate those troubles. Sketch the ideas that appeal to you as they would look applied to your grounds. Stare hard with squinted eyes at the space you intend to fill with fence until you are settled in your mind that the idea will work harmoniously with your architecture and with the neighborhood. It's not a bad idea to have in mind also the kinds of plants, shrubs, trees, vines or espaliers that will grow in front of or against this proposed fence.

Constructing the Board Fence

1. Mark the line of the fence and post placement—6 to 8 feet apart on center. See chapter 2, "Fence Posts," for details on marking out fence lines.

2. Dado the posts for the rails—generally 2 x 4s—that will carry the board siding.

3. Dig the holes and set the posts as shown in chapter 2.

4. Nail the rails in place with galvanized nails. If the fence is higher than 6 feet, use three rails for extra strength, and place the third one at about two-thirds of the fence height instead of midway between the top and bottom rails—this proportion is more pleasing to our eyes.

5. Nail on the siding with galvanized nails, then stain or paint the fence as you like.

You can make the fence a stronger, more massive structure by scaling up the timbers—use 8 x 8 posts, 4 x 4 rails and big 2-inch planks for siding. There are gardens where such a stately, solid fence looks right, and gives a mood of dignity and permanence.

The Post-and-Rail Fence

Post-and-rail fencing covers every style from the timber-hungry Virginia zig-zag and the variant post-and-rider to the crude rip-gut fences made of gnarled, twisted deadwood. The more sophisticated and thrifty type of post-and-rail fence is the mortised post (a post with holes made to receive the rails) with inserted rails. In the old days when these were working fences, they carried six and more rails set 4 inches apart. Today you can buy skimpy two-rail prefabricated fence kits that do little more than let the neighbors know you can afford to buy some fencing. Anything smaller than a camel can squeeze through the roomy gap between the rails of these fences. Nor is this fencing cheap; each post and each rail costs from five to seven dollars. If you have post and rail material in the raw on your property or growing in the region, you can build the fence of your dreams for less cash and a lot more labor.

The most common post-and-rail fence is simply a line of mortised posts with overlapping or neatly tenoned rails slipped into each mortise. The standard rail length is still 11 feet, and an average post size is 5 inches in diameter. If you plan to sit on the top rail and whittle,

Step 1. Mason's Twine Chalk Mark Plumb Bob Nail through Plastic Mark Post Placement 6'-8'

Step 2. Dado Posts A. Mark B. Saw C. Chisel

Step 3. Dig Holes Set Posts

Step 4. Place Rails 12" Step 5. Nail on Siding

A solid board fence can transform a noisy, exposed yard into a peaceful, secret retreat. Because of the expense and permanence of such a structure, good planning and consultation with neighbors are needed before the project is begun.

Step 1. Mark Mortises

Step 2. Drill Holes

Step 3. Chisel Out Mortises

Finished Mortise

The mortise and tenon is a basic joint, much used in timber framing and in sturdy fence construction. The mortise and tenon joint needs no nails and is very strong.

the tenoned rail is more likely to split than the overlapped.

Mortising a Post

1. Lay the post across two sawhorses and mark all the mortises with a carpenter's pencil.

2. Drill holes all around the inner perimeter of the mortise with a wide bit. Knock out the center.

3. Clean out the mortise with a wood chisel and hammer. Prepare all the posts before setting them in the ground, of course.

Overlapped rails rest on one another in the mortises. Usually such rails are tapered at the ends to avoid huge, post-weakening mortises. One reason for tenoning rails is to keep the mortises petite.

Tenoning a Rail

1. Mark each end of the rail line A to B the diameter of the post; that is, if you are fitting the rail into a 5-inch post, line A to B will

be 5 inches. Draw a straight horizontal line—B to B—across the butt end of the rail. Use a square and draw a line from B to C.

2. Saw through the rail from A down to C until the cut is level with line B to B across the butt face.

3. Set a wide chisel or a wedge along line B to B and strike it smartly with a hammer—the unwanted section will fall away. Trim it flat and level with the chisel and hammer. Repeat on the other end, and for the rest of the rails.

4. Fit the rails together in the mortise.

The Grapestake or Sapling Fence

A beautiful and popular California fence is the rough, weathered grapestake fence of split redwood which gives privacy and a handsome natural background for garden beds. Redwood stakes are expensive in the East, and thousands

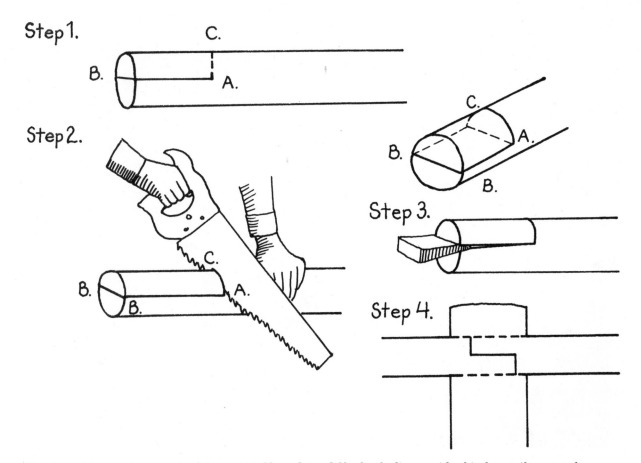

Overlapped tenons in a mortised fence post. If you have difficulty finding a wide chisel to strike away the unwanted wood in step 3, an axe or hatchet can be used. BE SURE TO WEAR SAFETY GLASSES. Striking metal against metal can send tiny but razor-sharp splinters flying. Best are wide wood chisels with a striking surface or handle of material made to take hammer blows.

of nails are needed to make a fence from the slender 2-inch stakes. Where the stakes are available at a moderate cost—west of the Rockies—they make fine fencing. Easterners can console themselves with peeled saplings of decay-resistant wood for a similar effect. The bark of the saplings must be peeled off or they will rot, harbor insects and not last long.

1. Cut and peel as many saplings of the right height as you need, or buy grapestakes. Saplings peel most easily in springtime. Most grapestakes today are split redwood sapwood, not the more desirable split heartwood.

2. Set 4 x 4 dadoed posts 2 or more feet in the ground along the fence line. Set them 6 to 8 feet apart on center.

3. Nail in the railings with galvanized nails, and set the top rail 6 to 12 inches below the height of the fence.

4. Nail the saplings or grapestakes in place. This is an easier job to do when the saplings are still green.

Both grapestakes and saplings make a rough, rural sort of "picket" fence that looks very well around the vegetable garden, for pickets don't have to be flat little boards. If you are clearing saplings from an overgrown meadow or thinning out a grove, keep future fencing possibilities in mind and set useful material aside. Be sure to debark the saplings and store them in a dry, shady place until they're needed. Larch saplings make excellent rustic trellises for grapevines, flowers and climbing vegetables.

The Chain-Link Fence

Chain-link is a useful but depressingly ugly fencing material that conjures up visions of dismal factories and detention camps. No one would choose chain-link for its aesthetic value, but for security purposes it cannot be beaten. If you keep a dog, a chain-link kennel is a good way to keep Old Bright-Eyes happy, comfortable and *at home*. Free-running dogs are a real headache in the country—they chase deer and kill the

The grapestake or sapling fence for privacy and for shading garden plants.

neighbors' chickens among many other sins—and are unlawful in most communities. Yet chaining a dog to a dog house year in and year out is pretty depressing both to owner and animal. A chain-link kennel lets sunshine, fresh air, and all the interesting sights in, and still gives the dog some illusion of freedom.

The fence is less obtrusive, and no more expensive, if you order the kind coated with colored vinyl. You can order an unassembled kennel kit that comes with a door and all the hardware, but these are usually quite small, rarely larger than 10 feet by 4 feet. If you buy the fencing, posts and door separately, you can put a larger kennel together for less money. A 10-foot by 15-foot enclosure that you make yourself will cost about the same as the smaller kennel kit.

The frame for a chain-link kennel consists of galvanized steel tubing posts of a diameter from 1⅝ inches to 2½ inches. These posts *must be set in concrete* at least 2½ feet deep. They can be more widely spaced than wooden posts—up to 10 feet apart on center.

The corner posts, which take the most stress,

should be at least 2 inches in diameter, as should the posts that take the gate. A top rail, fastened to the links with loop caps, is installed to give the structure rigidity at the top. Flat metal tension bars are then slipped into the ends of each section of link fence. Before the fencing is cut, it is stretched taut with a heavy-duty fence stretcher and stretcher chain. The tension bands that hold the fence section to the posts are then bolted in place, securing the post to the tension bar. As a final step, each end or corner post gets a cap.

The fence stretcher is the only special tool needed to erect a chain-link fence. Both Sears and Montgomery Ward as well as many fencing material dealers offer chain-link fencing and will lend (with a hefty deposit) the tools needed to do the job right. But you can use an ordinary come-along to stretch the fencing.

Gates for chain-link fencing come in many sizes and shapes, ready-made and complete with fittings, all set to mount on the gate posts. If you don't really need the strength of the chain-link gate, you can save 50 dollars or more by building a wooden door.

Step 1. Set Posts

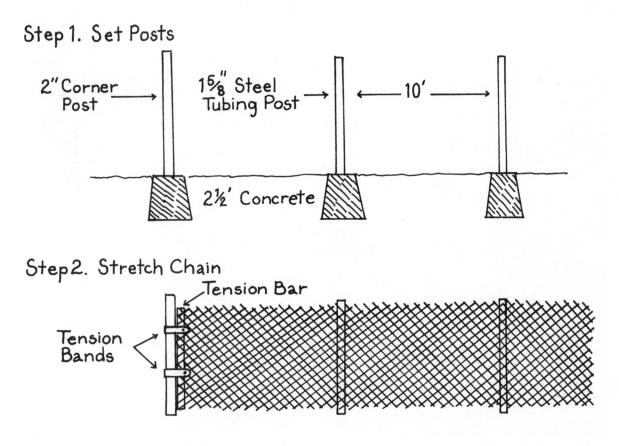

2" Corner Post

1⅝" Steel Tubing Post

← 10' →

2½' Concrete

Step 2. Stretch Chain

Tension Bar

Tension Bands

Step 3. Attach Top Rail

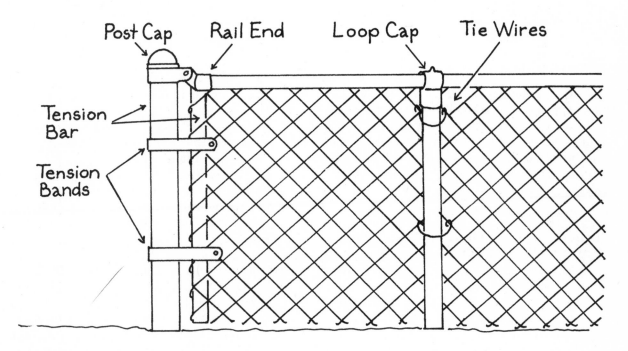

Post Cap

Rail End

Loop Cap

Tie Wires

Tension Bar

Tension Bands

The chain-link fence is useful where security is important. The special tools for putting up chain-link fencing can be rented from fencing dealers or from rental businesses.

Special Project
Building a Dog-Run

Decide on an ample size (make the kennel as large as you can afford) so that the dog can get exercise. Situate the kennel and dog house in a sheltered area where snow drifting is at a minimum. Low, wet ground is a pretty undesirable place for the structure. Good drainage, sunshine and shade should be available to the animal.

1. Lay out the fence lines with stakes and twine, marking the post positions on center, 6 to 10 feet apart.
2. Dig the post holes, mix the concrete and set the posts. Let the concrete set undisturbed for at least two days before attaching the chain-link fencing.
3. Never pre-cut sections of chain-link fencing; it's very easy to miscalculate the amount of stretch. Fasten one end of a section onto a post with tension bands after you have slipped a tension bar in place through the linkage.
4. Unroll the fencing, and attach the fence stretcher and stretcher chain following the directions that come with the tools you are using. Pull the fencing taut.
5. Slip the tension bar for this end through the links, then bolt the section to the post with the tension bands; when all is secure, cut the fencing. Follow this procedure for each section.
6. Continue around the kennel until all the fence sections are snugly mounted. Fasten on the top rail and add the post caps.
7. If you buy a chain-link gate to go with your kennel, it will come with female hinges and drop fork latches. Don't forget to purchase male hinges to fit the outside diameter of your posts. Simply bolt them in place and hang the gate from them.

CHAPTER 4

GATES

There are thousands of gate designs, from crude but workable bar gates in cow yards to elaborate wrought-iron, lattice-work, or jigsaw-cut-work gates. Sometimes big driveway gates are mounted on a heavy castor or runner wheel where snowfall is negligible and driveways are paved. But too often garden gates and entrance gates to the front walk are built and hung by the weekend handyman who thinks enthusiasm is an effective substitute for know-how. It is not. However, the rules for making a sturdy gate are not difficult to master, and if you follow them you can have a gate that will remain useful and attractive for many years.

Avoiding Gate Problems

Posts Skimpy posts set shallow will lean as the weight of the gate pulls inexorably upon them. Use stout, substantial posts—6 x 6s or even 8 x 8s—and set them at least 3 feet deep. Out-of-plumb posts lick you before you start. Plumb posts are a necessity for a straight gate.

Hinges Small hinges spaced far apart will gradually pull loose as the gate is opened and shut, opened and shut. The gate sags a trifle then, putting more strain on the hinges; then they give a little more. The reciprocal action ends with the gate off its bottom hinge and hanging by a thread at the top. Always use the *biggest* hinges that will fit on the gate. And if the gate is a heavy one, don't be stingy with the hinges—use three or four.

Weight Massive gates look fine for a little while, until they start to droop and drag in the dirt. The force of gravity and its own weight will pull a heavy gate down. Gates should always be built as light as possible. If you must use heavy timbers for a gate, think about a double-door design to distribute the weight on another set of hinges.

Bracing Everybody knows a gate should be braced, but not everybody knows how and where to brace. The brace must always point up and away from the hinges. Instead of a wooden brace, you can use a heavy wire that can be tightened with a turnbuckle if the gate starts to sag.

Constructing a Basic Gate

This gate is good for garden, entrance, poultry yard, field, driveway, patio or a dozen other places, depending on its size and style. The basic principles are the same. (See illustration on page 38.)

1. Measure the fence opening for the gate. If the opening is out of plumb, do everything possible to correct the situation before building a gate. A crooked opening means a sagging, troublesome gate. You may have to reset a leaning post. Assure yourself that the posts can carry the weight of the gate you plan. If the posts are too flimsy, you have two choices: set heavier posts in place before going on, or design a lighter gate.

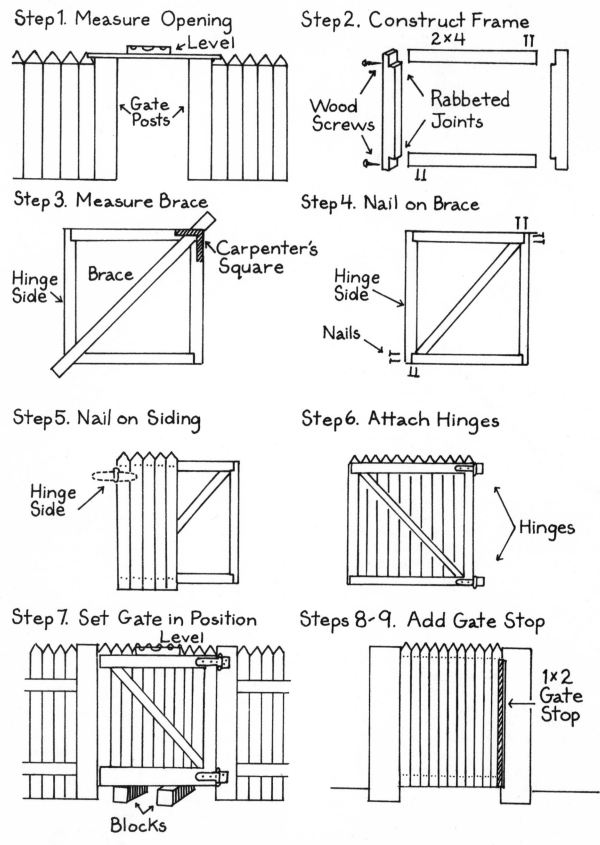

Step 1. Measure Opening

Level

Gate Posts

Step 2. Construct Frame

2×4

Wood Screws

Rabbeted Joints

Step 3. Measure Brace

Carpenter's Square

Hinge Side

Brace

Step 4. Nail on Brace

Hinge Side

Nails

Step 5. Nail on Siding

Hinge Side

Step 6. Attach Hinges

Hinges

Step 7. Set Gate in Position

Level

Blocks

Steps 8-9. Add Gate Stop

1×2 Gate Stop

Just as a chain is only as strong as its weakest link, a fence is only as strong as its gate. Many good home craftsmen who build a fine fence come to grief with the gate, setting the brace backward or using hinges too small for the weight of the gate. Good alignment, correct bracing, and big hinges mean a strong, level gate.

Allow ½ inch for hinge clearance and another ½ inch for latch clearance in your measurements. Write the measurements down.

2. Be extremely picky about the lumber for the gate. Choose unwarped, well-seasoned, dry lumber. Straight, dry 2 x 4s will do well for the Z-frame brace. Cut the frame pieces first, but do not cut the brace yet. Nailed butt joints are fine for lesser projects, but a gate deserves rabbeted joints fastened with wood screws. (In a butt joint, the two pieces of wood are merely pushed together and held in contact by some sort of fastener. In a rabbeted joint, one piece is rabbeted, that is, notched across the grain, and the other is fitted into the notch.) Using a carpenter's square, check the squareness of the frame as you put the members together, and check again when all four sections are joined.

3. Lay down the 2 x 4 that will serve as the brace, and place the squared gate frame on top of it, corner to corner, up and away from where the bottom hinge will be set. Mark the

Another Way to Frame the Gate

This is not quite as rugged a gate as the rabbeted frame gate, but as a low-use garden door it will give good service, and it has the advantage of being light and easier to build. It is particularly well suited to the picket fence.

1. Measure the gate opening as for the rabbeted frame gate, and use care in choosing dry, unwarped lumber.

2. Cut 2 x 4s for the top and bottom rails of the gate and lay them out on a flat surface at the correct distance for the gate.

3. Using a carpenter's square, position the end pickets on the rails so they are square and plumb, and form the side frame of the gate. Nail them in place with galvanized nails, and recheck for squareness.

4. Turn the frame over. Measure and cut the 2 x 4 brace to fit between the bottom hinge-side rail and the diagonal corner.

5. Secure the brace to the top and bottom rails with 4-inch wood screws about 2 inches from each end as shown.

6. Finish the gate by nailing the rest of the pickets to the rails and the brace. Set the hinge straps on the rails.

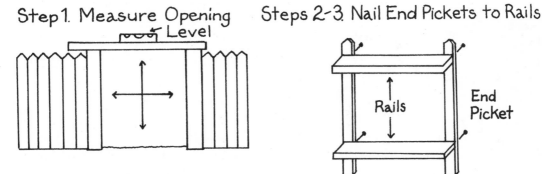

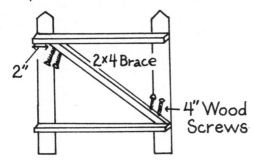

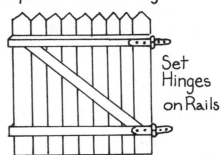

Another way to build a gate is to use the end pickets as an integral part of the frame.

2 x 4 with a pencil. Cut the 2 x 4 outside the pencil mark. This will be a tight fit—you may have to tap the brace into place with a hammer before nailing it.

4. Nail the brace in place horizontally and vertically.

5. Nail on the siding, whether board, picket or rail, starting from the hinge side.

6. Attach the hinges to the gate first. Use the longest screws the wood will take without being pierced. Pre-drill the screw holes with a bit one size smaller than the screws.

7. Set the gate in the opening on blocks so that it is in the right position and level as well as plumb. Mark where the hinges are to go on the post, pre-drill the holes, then attach the hinges, allowing enough room for the gate to swing freely.

8. Use any sort of latch you like—thumb latch, bolt latch, top latch, ring latch or hasp latch.

9. Nail a gate stop onto the latch post by running a strip of 1 x 2 up the post so the gate may butt up against it. This keeps it from swinging past the arc of the hinges.

Repairing a Sagging Gate

The sag can come from two sources—a leaning post or a poorly braced gate. The remedy is simple. For a leaning post, get ⅛-inch-diameter stainless-steel cable, a 7¾-inch turnbuckle with ⅜-inch eyes, and four cable clamps. You will also need two ⅜-inch eyebolts long enough to go through the posts.

1. Set the eyebolts into the posts as shown.
2. Cut the cable into two sections and fasten one end of each section to the eyebolts with the cable clamps.
3. Fasten the other ends to each end of the turnbuckle.
4. Tighten the turnbuckle by turning it with a stout screwdriver until the post is upright.

A poorly braced gate can be squared up the same way, by running the cable from the bottom hinge side of the gate to the diagonal corner, just as you would a wooden brace. Tighten the turnbuckle to square up the gate.

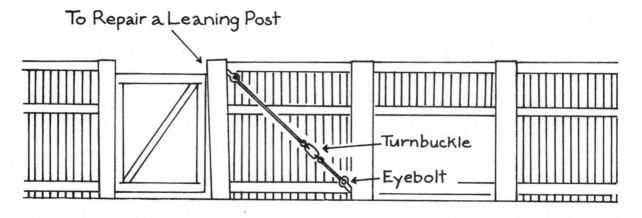

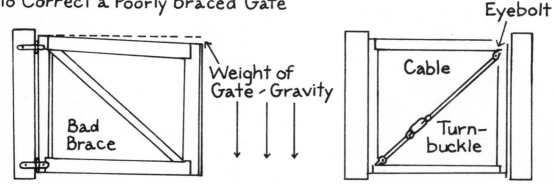

Leaning posts and bad gate bracing are the most common gate problems. Both can be corrected with a cable and turnbuckle.

CHAPTER 5 _____

FENCELIKE STRUCTURES—TRELLISES, ARBORS AND PERGOLAS

A century ago, nearly every backyard had some kind of structure to support gracefully looping vines and rose climbers, or to provide a shady spot in which to sit and visit away from the house, amid the sights and scents of a flourishing garden. These are pleasant candidates for revival today.

The Trellis

The word "trellis" means only one thing to too many people—a flimsy, fan-shaped structure painted white and stuck in the middle of grandmother's lawn behind a rambler rose. There is the dim and fleeting memory of an attractive fan-shaped spray of roses, then the sadder but more lasting image of a rampant rose burying the trellis beneath its weight until the structure leans, falls and at last lies vanquished on the ground, never to rise again. The fan trellis was not meant to be free-standing, but to rest against a house or wall. If a trellis is going to support a heavy climbing vine over a period of years, it should be built strong and sturdy and should be incorporated into an existing structure like a building, wall or fence.

Trellises are extremely versatile structures, one of the gardener's most potent weapons against the monotony of the square, flat backyard. An arched trellis over a gate, crested

with perfumed flowers and leaves, is an enchanting entranceway to a home or a garden. A trellised bower with a seat inside at the end of the garden offers a pleasant goal for an evening stroll through the beds of flowers and vegetables. Fragrant flowered vines make such a retreat even more enticing. Trellises have an honorable place in the vegetable garden, too, as supports for cucumbers, gourds, tomatoes and even melons, allowing you to send rambling, ground-hogging plants up the trellis vertically. Trellises seem to work best with lighter plants and annuals where a summer's worth of color and bloom is what is wanted, or where rambling vegetables must be contained.

To make a lightweight movable tomato and cucumber trellis that will be put away at the end of the summer, use decay-resistant cedar posts (the more spindly posts of 2-inch diameter) and lath supports. You can drive the pointed ends of the cedar stakes into the ground with a maul.

Another functional garden trellis is the hinged A-frame, no wider than 3 feet, and about 4 feet tall.

If you want to help a climbing vine, whether morning glory or silver fleece, up a wall, a simple frame of preservative-treated 2 x 4s with decay-resistant heartwood cross members can be quickly built and hung on storm sash hangers against a building wall.

The Climbing Rose Clothesline-Post Trellis

Our backyards are full of utilitarian but unattractive things—garbage cans, oil tanks, gas tanks, telephone poles, power pole anchor cables and clotheslines. All of these can be concealed behind lattice-work or simple lath trellises, which allow vines to grow where they won't get in the way. Morning glories on the telephone pole, a hop vine on the anchor cable and a climbing rose on your clothesline posts don't get in the way, add vertical color and interest to the backyard, and help disguise what they cover. Add beauty wherever you can. It makes any job more pleasant.

To make hanging out the clothes a trip to a rose garden, build a simple 2 x 4 preservative-treated frame and ladder it with horizontal laths. Set it at the end of the clothesline T-support, plant a rambler rose and enjoy a fragrant result. (You can do this at each end of the clothesline.) If the rambunctious rose starts to grow along the clothesline, keep it in bounds with a pair of nippers.

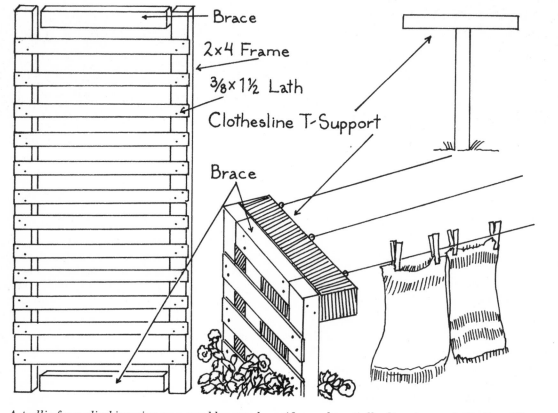

A trellis for a climbing vine or a rambler rose beautifies and partially disguises a clothesline. The imaginative use of trellises and climbing plants can transform many unattractive backyard structures into rosy, fragrant bowers—an arched trellis over the trash can bin, a trellis against a stark new exterior wall.

The Arbor

An arbor is a colonnade, sometimes with latticed sides over which vines and climbing plants may grow to form a tunnel of greenery, fruit and flower. Grape arbors are favorites of the home gardener, but many are built too small and rickety. New-built arbors are frequently painted white, but in a few years the grapevines twist over and around the arbor and the scaling, cracked paint cannot be freshened up or reap-

plied without ripping down the vines. Grape-vines can live for half a century, and once they're growing you don't move them. A grape arbor should therefore be made of fairly heavy timbers of decay-resistant wood that will weather naturally and last the life of the vine. Grape-vines are usually planted about 8 feet apart, so the arbor must be a decent length unless you have only two or four vines. Since the vines must be pruned annually, don't build the arbor so high that you cannot get at the vines with a step ladder.

You may prefer to grow clematis, wisteria or trumpet vine up and over your arbor. Whatever climbers you plan to use with the arbor, design the structure so that the plants can get their full complement of sunlight.

For an arbor, use 4 x 4 posts 10 feet long, and 2 x 4 rafters and beams. Use preservative-treated lumber that will not harm plants. You can nail or bolt the arbor members together with galvanized fasteners; galvanized metal connectors at key points will hold the super-structure firmly and lastingly together to make the arbor a safe and attractive structure for generations, pleasant for walking under, convenient for the grape grower or gardener, and good for the vines. (See illustration page 44.)

1. Figure the size of the arbor and the direction of its axis based on the needs of the vines you intend to plant along it. Lay out the lines as you would for a fence. Mark the post placement.

2. Set the posts 3 feet deep, allowing 7 feet above ground.

3. Set the beams in place, and bolt or nail them to the posts. Add insurance with galvanized metal connectors.

4. Nail the rafters in place with galvanized nails.

Step 1. Mark Post Placement

10' Posts - Preservative Treated

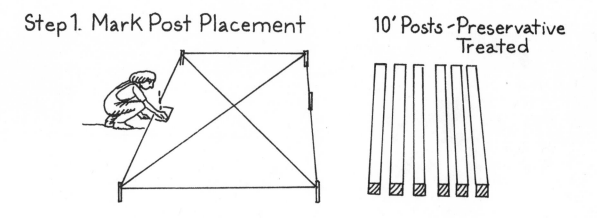

Steps 2-3. Set Posts and Beams in Place

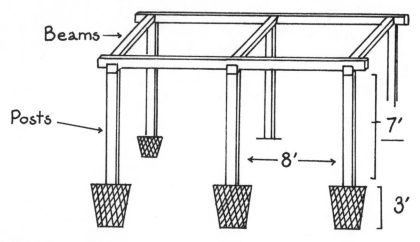

Beams →

Posts →

7'

8'

3'

Step 4. Nail on Rafters

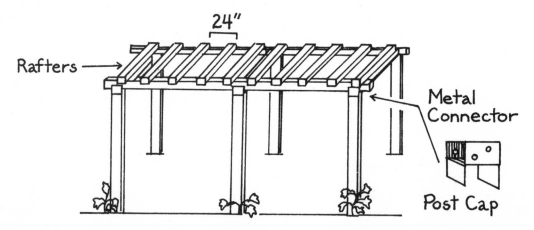

24"

Rafters →

Metal Connector

Post Cap

A crucial factor in arbor construction is to make it big enough and strong enough to carry the weight of heavy climbing vines for many years, for most arbor vines, particularly grapes, cannot be moved without damaging the plant if repairs to the structure become necessary.

The Pergola

The pergola is a marvelous Italian invention that has greater architectural weight than an arbor. A strong structure with an open roof of large timbers, it can carry heavy vines such as grape, clematis or wisteria. A pergola is like an oversized arbor with open sides; generally the vines climb the posts and arch overhead to make a roof of foliage and bloom. Pergolas are often built over patios where the vines eventually make a shady wall and roof. If your backyard calls for a pergola instead of an arbor, use 6 x 6 posts set 3 feet deep, 4 x 4 rafters and 6 x 6 beams. Galvanized metal connectors are essential to keep such an ambitious structure rigid and sturdy. Bolted T-ties will keep post and beam solid and prevent side sway. The building codes of most communities have something to say about such heavy structures as pergolas: they insist that the rafters be connected to a 2 x 6 ledger lag-bolted to an existing house wall. This is why you so often see pergolas in modern gardens fastened to the side of a house rather than free-standing as they were in their Italian beginnings.

2
WALKWAYS AND PATIOS OF BRICK AND FLAGSTONE
plus Edgings and Walls

CHAPTER 6

THE TRADITION OF BRICK WALKS AND TERRACES

Every gardener has a dream landscape, and for some of us it is composed of a mellow brick walk dappled with coins of sunlight and leading to a sunny garden enclosed by an old brick wall. Against the wall a grapevine grows and vegetable, herb and flower beds are linked by edged pathways of paving brick in subtle earth colors. Such a brick-ornamented garden is as old as civilization; it was already an ancient idea when the Romans laid their brick walkways through the estate gardens of the wealthy in the countryside and was the traditional style in medieval cloistered courtyards, gardens and walkways. Even the secret gardens of the East were locked behind high brick walls, often worked in fanciful and elaborate bond patterns enriched with polychrome glazed tiles.

Wood and stone are natural materials that need reshaping or careful selection before they can be used in building, but bricks are a human invention whose shape and size fit the human hand, and their versatile modular dimensions are easy to work with and delight our eyes whether in a wall or a walkway.

The familiar red brick used in buildings gives structures a certain tranquillity. Brick takes the afternoon sunlight well and casts an old rose light on dull and sleety days. Sometimes the only touch of color in a drab November landscape is the subtle warmth of a brick house.

People have been making bricks for thousands of years, from the crude pre-historic sundried bricks to the exquisite enameled bricks made by the ancient Assyrians and Babylonians, to the modern variety of bricks in more than ten thousand sizes, shapes and textures. Connoisseurs of brickwork cite the ancient Persian mosques, their mosaic brick and glazed tiles in extraordinarily rich green-blues, ochres and lustrous pearl shimmering in colorful radiance, as the aesthetic peak of brick manufacture.

The invention of "burnt" brick—clay brick shapes fired in a kiln until they became hard, brittle and strong—was a tremendous architectural advance. Burnt bricks allowed thinner walls than the old adobe sun-dried blocks, and made it easier to build structures with ruler-straight lines. They gave the builder an architectural control of the material that eventually led to vaulting and imaginative geometric forms.

In this country during the colonial period bricks were imported from Holland and England until the domestic brick industry slowly began producing burnt bricks in volume. Yet there were very early brickyards, perhaps the first one set up in Henrico, Virginia (near what is now Richmond), in 1611 under the advice of Sir Thomas Dale, acting governor of the Virginia Colony. The brick resisted the damp climate well, and there are hints that bricks were

49

made at home on the farm, for the bricks used in a Smithfield farmhouse built in 1630 show the footprints of dogs and chickens in them. Up in New Amsterdam the Dutch also set up a brick kiln early on, and most of the houses in that trading town were built of good New World brick. No examples of homemade brick buildings still stand, but old pictures show their rich details, stepped gables and ornamental bonds. Albany became especially famous for excellent brick. An ingenious labor-saving method used in colonial times to soften the clay from which bricks were made was to drive a herd or two of cows through the clay bed until the material was malleable.

Imported bricks were used for the finest buildings. Dutch bricks, perfected by a people who lacked a natural stone supply, were of the highest quality and much esteemed. Along the Hudson River in former Dutch settlements, elegant houses built of these imported bricks still stand, sometimes with attached garden walls. By 1650 burnt bricks were being made in New England, and 50 years later there were so many operating brickyards that New England ships were deep into the brick trade, carrying loads of fine New England brick over the seas. Perhaps the most extraordinary brickwork in the country was executed in Philadelphia when that city was the cultural center of the New World; the Philadelphia style of building so evoked eighteenth-century London that English visitors always felt curiously at home there.

For gardeners then and now, bricks are a tremendously versatile material with dozens of uses—garden and bed edging, walkways, garden and retaining walls, patios, sturdy compost bins, tree wells, niched seats in walls. The effect of brick in the garden and yard is one of natural mellow warmth, neatness and permanence. Many gardeners are more comfortable working with brick instead of flagstone because the uniform shapes are easy to handle and do not require fussing and pondering over a vast pile of rocks. Bricks are small and light, and anyone can work with them.

Old Brick

Old bricks—chipped, weathered and stained—are as eagerly sought by gardeners as rare bulbs and swamp orchids. Decades ago when gardening was pursued mostly on the estates of the wealthy or by eccentrics, and the Amer-

ican passion for the vast blank green lawn was at its most intense, old brick could be had cheaply or even free for the carting. This writer remembers 20 years ago getting free truckloads of old brick from a bank destroyed by fire. Of course, all the mortar had to be chipped off the brick surfaces and each brick cleaned up with a wire brush—a long and dreary task that took a whole summer's worth of odd hours. But the long garden path that came from the work was a delight. In the days when burned buildings left a blackened chimney thrusting starkly into the air, the owners were glad to have some gardener offer to pull the thing down and take the bricks away. No more! Used brick today costs nearly as much as new brick, and is in great demand by many people, including thousands of gardeners who have discovered the pleasures of using it in their own backyard landscaping. Although old brick is more fragile and harder to work with than new, and almost always has to be cleaned of lumpy old mortar, it's worth all that for its glowing, mellow beauty.

The how-to books on bricklaying solemnly warn against using old brick, for it is structurally weaker than new, and, they say, will not

Cleaning Old Bricks

Cleaning the mortar off bricks from an old chimney or building is a slow, rather tedious job best done in short stretches of spare time. Very old bricks are not too difficult to clean, for the rotten mortar usually breaks away with the tap of a rock hammer. In addition to a rock hammer or geologist's hammer, you will need a cold chisel, a wire brush and a stout pair of leather gloves.

1. Dampen the bricks and mortar thoroughly and often with a hose, or let a few bricks soak in a bucket while you work on others. Wetting them down softens the mortar and helps it break away from the bricks more easily, as well as keeping the irritating dust to a minimum.

2. Chip the mortar off each brick with oblique, moderate hammer blows or with the hammer and chisel. Restrain any impulse to hit the brick hard; too smart a blow may break it.

3. Vigorous scrubbing with a wire brush finishes the job. Stack the cleaned bricks to one side—don't toss them in a pile, as quite a few could break from the impact.

present a nice uniformity of color and texture. "Quite right!" cries the gardener on this aesthetic point, and goes on enthusiastically grubbing old brick out of ancient rubbish heaps. It's probably not a bad idea to use new brick in any wall more than 2 feet high, but old brick in a low bed wall or a walk or terrace floor is beautiful, with its mottled, varicolored earth hues. And a few seconds after the last brick is set, such a structure looks like it has been there a hundred years. The monotonous one-color look of a batch of hard new brick is just what we don't want. Some brick makers and specialty building supply dealers (the same people, no doubt, who sell new "weathered barn boards")

have noticed the appeal of old brick and produce new bricks that look stained and weathered, and are of varied colors. Other dealers handle used brick that is cleaned and all ready to use, but at a fearful price.

New Brick

New bricks come in so many forms, sizes and textures it's impossible to list them all. They can be striated, stippled, smooth, grooved or sand-finished; they can be molded, hollowed or notched; they come in red, purple, white and ochre; their sizes range from common to jumbo,

Common Brick

Adobe Brick

Cored Brick

Paving Brick

Interlocking Pavers

Turf Block

Brick is one of mankind's most versatile building materials, and it comes in thousands of different shapes, colors, forms and functions. Try to suit the brick to the project.

from thin pavers to thick blocks. Some bricks are expressly made for inside use, and others for outdoors in harsh climates where they will be exposed to the most severe weather.

Adobe Brick and Burnt Brick

There are two basic sorts of brick—sun-dried or *adobe* brick, one of our most ancient building materials, and *burnt* brick, which has been subjected to high temperatures in a brick kiln.

Adobe bricks are made of sand, clay and some plant fiber material such as chopped straw or moss. This plant material binds the brick and lets it dry and shrink without cracking. Adobe bricks are hardened by drying and curing in the hot sun where the humidity is low. Although adobe is often thought of as the native architecture of our Southwest, it was not greatly used there, according to one architectural authority, until the Spanish conquistadores brought the style up from Mexico. Recent studies have shown that the so-called adobe soil of the Southwest is actually too high in clay content to make the best adobe bricks.

Large adobe bricks weigh 30 to 50 pounds each, making them difficult to handle and impossible to ship farther than local distances without shooting the cost sky-high, which is also the case with burnt bricks. Since there are very few commercial sources of natural adobe brick, making it has become very much a do-it-yourself project, though it is a beautiful and desirable building material in the Southwest and particularly in the San Joaquin Valley in California. Traditional adobe is not a good material where the rainfall goes over the "scarce" marker, for the bricks are softened by moisture and can collapse in severe downpours. It is discouraging to builders in this handsome regional style to make the bricks and build a wall or house, only to have the structure melt into mud in the rain. Fortunately, a recent treatment of adobe brick mixtures with an asphalt emulsion have made a sturdier, waterproof block with nearly the same strength and weather-enduring qualities as burnt brick.

Adobe makes exquisite garden walls. It is laid like mortared brick, with the mortar struck off flush with the block faces for the solid, massy, organic feeling of this local style. Some adobe walls are plastered and painted to make a more homogeneous background, but the most beautiful are left in their natural earth colors. Adobe patios and garden walks with their subtle shadings of tones make the material one of the most striking outdoor patio surfaces.

If you want to make your own adobe brick, there are two excellent sources of information about the rather complicated process. The Department of Housing Technology, California State University, Fresno, CA 93726, has published detailed directions for making your own adobe blocks, including methods for adding asphalt emulsions to waterproof them. A more complete treatment is found in Duane Newcomb's *The Owner-Built Adobe House*. The undertaking is quite laborious and lengthy, but reportedly as satisfying as building your own stone wall.

If you want to make adobe blocks for an aboveground structure, whether garden wall or house, you *must* have precisely the right soil mixtures or the blocks will be too fragile and apt to crack. California building codes insist that homemade adobe blocks pass a laboratory stress test before they can be used, and the block maker pays for the test. However, making your own adobe for a patio floor or a low garden wall (under 3 feet high) is a worthwhile project if you live in the Southwest, have room enough for scores of drying blocks, and can take weeks of work molding and curing the blocks properly. Envious Easterners should not try to make adobe blocks—we simply have too much humidity in the atmosphere for adobe to ever dry out properly.

Burnt bricks are made of various common earth clays which are plastic and whose particles cling to each other when they are wet. When the clay brick is heated or fired in a kiln, it becomes brittle and rigid, and undergoes a molecular change which prevents it from taking up water again except mechanically.

There are hundreds of brickyards all over the country, for the weight of the bricks and the fairly common occurrence of suitable clays make local manufacture and distribution economical and practical. The color of the clay is rarely the warm familiar red of the common fired brick, for the color change occurs when the iron content of the clay oxidizes under heat to make iron oxide, which is red. Light-colored rose and salmon bricks are underfired. Such bricks are relatively weak and porous, and are used mostly for facings with sturdier bricks behind them. Bricks that have been fired hard are dark and often have a purplish cast. These are very strong and impervious to water.

If you want to use brick for a garden wall, edging, walkway or outdoor flooring, the brick men advise using bricks that can withstand weather. The manufacturers' specifications grade bricks according to their weather resistance. SW brick resists Severe Weathering with repeated frost and thaws. MW can take only Moderate Weathering, while NW—No Weathering—is for inside use only. If bricks are in contact with the ground, they should be SW for long life and stability.

Special paving bricks for walks and patios come in dozens of sizes, colors and shapes, including hexagons and squares as well as the familiar rectangles. Paving bricks have a smooth but not slippery surface, are SW rated, and are usually thinner than common bricks, since they are set in a bed of mortar or sand. Sometimes you can go down to the brickyard, if there is one nearby, and get sub-grade brick at a bargain price. This inferior brick cannot be used for building construction, but does good service in the garden.

Brick Sizes

Brick usually comes in modular sizes, which means the dimensions are simple multiples of each other: two bricks set sideways equal one brick set longways. This allows them to be put together in many different patterns by variously arranging them on their edges, sides and

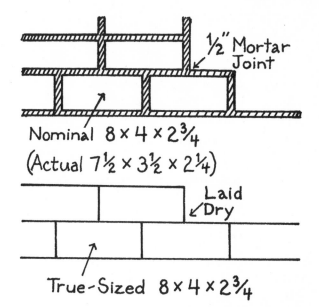

Common bricks are nominal or true. Patio floors laid without mortar call for true bricks. Mortared walls or patios must be built of nominal bricks.

backs to form diamonds, herringbones, stacks and the handsome Flemish and English bonds.

Brick sizes can be *nominal* or *true*. A nominal common brick is said to be 8 inches by 4 inches by 2¾ inches, but this figure includes a standard ½-inch mortar joint, so the brick actually measures 7½ inches by 3½ inches by 2¼ inches. If you are laying a patio or terrace floor dry—that is, without the use of mortar—you will want true or actual-size bricks whose dimensions are literally 8 inches by 4 inches by 2¾ inches, or pavers that are 8 inches by 4 inches by 1⅝ inches.

CHAPTER 7 ⎯⎯⎯⎯⎯⎯⎯⎯⎯⎯⎯⎯⎯⎯⎯⎯⎯⎯

PATIOS AND TERRACES

If you are dreaming about making a brick-floored patio joining your house and garden or inside the garden itself, don't get carried away by the illustrations in masonry and bricklaying books of vast paved areas called "garden patios" that, despite their name, have only a few miserable little circles or squares of earth let into the brickwork, each just large enough for one or two dwarf plants. If you are a gardener, you might be better pleased to stick to your rows and beds and plan to work in several small patios, each suited to a particularly choice view or prospect. Very tiny patios, big enough for only two chairs or a stone bench fitted cunningly into a fragrant bower or near the spring tulip display, or making a pleasant resting place adjoining the vegetable garden, will give your yard and grounds more interest and diversity than one large paved area. Two patios, perhaps linked by a walk, one sunny and warm for brisk spring and autumn days, one shaded and cool for the summer, are more intriguing and tempting to a garden stroller than the broad parking-lot sweep of the giant terrace. Planning where walkways and patios should go on your property takes considerable thought. A very useful small book is *New Budget Landscaping: Designing Your Outdoor Space for Use, Comfort, and Pleasure,* by Carlton B. Lees, the vice-president of the New York Botanical Garden and a well-known garden and landscape designer. The

book helps solve dozens of problem cases—the suburban house next to an orchard, the basic woodland backyard, the deep, narrow city backyard—and includes an imaginative list of trees, shrubs and climbing plants that will give every gardener hundreds of ideas. Do not neglect the plantsmens' catalogs which often group plants in landscaped settings that suggest walkway and patio placement. Outstanding are the catalogs of White Flower Farm, Litchfield, CT 06759, and Wayside Gardens, Hodges, SC 29695.

Dry or Mortared

Building a mortared brick patio takes precise measurements and alignments, a concrete slab, and a great deal of careful and skillful labor. It is an expensive project with no room for mistakes; such finicky work should be done by a skilled mason. If you really want a mortared patio, you should apprentice yourself out to a brick mason, and when you feel capable of taking on the job, follow the directions for materials, designs and specifications which are covered in fine detail in a series of technical bulletins on mortared brick patio and walkway construction. Write to: Brick Institute of America, 1750 Old Meadow Road, McLean, VA 22102.

A far better choice for the gardener is the flexible, dry-laid brick patio, particularly in the North where alternate freezing and thawing can crumble mortar and heave concrete slabs.

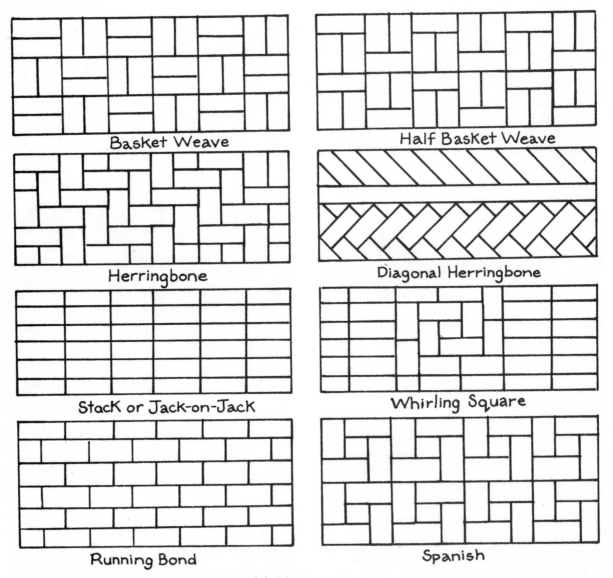

Basket Weave

Half Basket Weave

Herringbone

Diagonal Herringbone

Stack or Jack-on-Jack

Whirling Square

Running Bond

Spanish

Various types of bond patterns for paving with bricks.

True-sized bricks laid closely together on a bed of damp, level sand, make a sturdy, long-lasting surface that has the additional bonus of being easily removable if you decide later that a lily pond or a gazebo would be better in that spot. Individual bricks that break or get damaged can be handily replaced. A flexible terrace is easier to build, more forgiving of mistakes and repositioned bricks, and a good deal cheaper than the mortared kind. Fine sand is swept down into the joints of the dry terrace bricks several times over a period of weeks, and the tiny crystals interlock and bind the bricks tightly together. The sand is important, so don't be tempted to set patio bricks directly in the earth; they will wobble, heave and sink. A flexible brick patio bound only by sand needs a firm and solid border to lock the margin bricks firmly into place. Sometimes the border is set in concrete, but it can be sunk directly into the soil if the soil is a type that can be tamped hard and compact. Without a border, the bricks on the edge of the patio will loosen and fall away,

and the joints between the bricks farther into the center of the patio will gape and spread in time.

Certain paving patterns are better than others for the flexible patio, particularly the delightful herringbone and the running bond. Both of these knit the bricks firmly together. Stack bond (or jack-on-jack) is a poor choice for sand-set bricks because the pattern is not an interlocking system, but rows of separate units laid side by side, easily dislodged or heaved up to trip the unsuspecting walker. On the other hand, adobe patios are best set with stack bond and are hard to lay in an interlocking pattern because of the variation in sizes of the adobe blocks.

Estimating Quantities

Dry-laid flexible patios and walks are best built with true-sized bricks set snugly and tightly together.

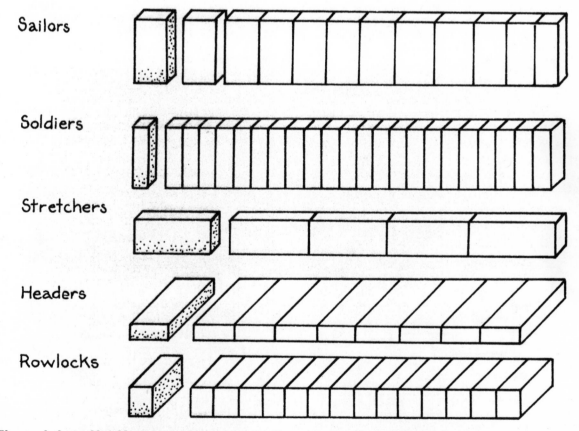

Sailors

Soldiers

Stretchers

Headers

Rowlocks

The vocabulary of bricklaying is richly descriptive. Here are a few ways of describing the positions in which bricks can be set.

1. Measure the area that is to be paved, either in feet or inches, depending on the size of the surface. If you measure by feet, multiply the length by the width to give you the square footage that is going to be covered. If you measure by inches—for a tiny area—multiply the width by the length and divide the result by 144 to get a square footage figure.

2. Figure how many bricks you will use for each square foot. This is best calculated by actually laying out several feet of brick in your chosen pattern or—second best—making a paper pattern. A 12-inch by 12-inch adobe paver will fill up a square foot by itself. True-sized bricks 8 inches by 4 inches take 4½ bricks to fill a square foot, but some patterns call for diagonally cut bricks that can make a fair percentage of waste. Multiply the square feet of the total area by the number of bricks per square foot you need, and you will have the basic number of bricks it will take for the paving.

3. Compute the number of bricks you need for the edging. First, add up the sides of the proposed patio for the perimeter measurement and convert the figure into inches. Decide how the bricks are to be set—upright sailors are a favorite, strong and good-looking. Divide the perimeter measurement by the number of edging inches spanned by one brick. The figure is the number of bricks you need for the edging, roughly 25 percent of the number needed for the patio.

Cutting Brick

Cutting bricks crosswise or diagonally is not difficult, and though the cut surface will be rough, the brick is perfectly good that way. You can dress the surface up a little with a chisel if you like.

Just as for cutting stone, wear goggles and gloves. Cut bricks with a brick set and hammer or a rented brick cutter.

1. Mark the line where you want the break to occur on the brick with a pencil.
2. Set the brick in sand and score it along the line by tapping the brick set handle with a hammer.

3. Now, with the good part of the brick toward you, set the brick set in the scored groove so that the beveled edge faces away from you. Give the brick set a smart smack with the hammer and the brick should obligingly part. If not, score again and try once more.

A brick cutter is a special guillotine with an adjustable blade that fits over a whole brick. It can be rented from a tool rental dealer. Using this device, a hearty whack with a 3-pound crack hammer cuts the brick without scoring.

Abrasive blades available for portable circular saws can be used to cut bricks. They are particularly good for cutting angles.

Brick Set

Scored Pencil Line

Brick Cutter

Brick

Blade

Two basic ways of cutting brick.

4. To the patio brick number and the edging brick number add 5 percent of the total for breakage and cutting waste.

Bricks are often sold in pre-packaged cubes of 500 or 1,000, and usually the price is a little softer if you buy them this way. A cube of bricks is very likely to be all one homogeneous color. Most brickyards tack a healthy delivery charge onto the price of the brick.

Before your bricks are delivered, pick a good spot for them to be unloaded, as near the project site as possible and in a place where the driver can get his truck in and out again without getting stuck. If the bricks are coming in a cube, build a simple platform of 2 x 4s and stout planks for the cube to be lowered onto. Don't let your bricks be dumped—they are brittle and the breakage can be considerable. If you've ordered an odd number of bricks, you may have to take them off the truck and stack them manually, so have some help on hand.

Constructing the Dry-Laid Patio

You will need: brick, a bed of coarse sand 2 inches deep over the area to be paved, fine sand for filling in between the cracks of the bricks, a screed, a level, 2 x 4s for temporary edging, a push broom, a shovel, a brick set, hammer and scrap lumber. A 4 x 4 tamper will help firm up the soil.

The whole area where your patio will lie should be dug out to a depth that will accommodate 2 inches of sand and the brick topping so that the finished patio will be level with the ground. A long session with the shovel, hoe, level and tamper may be needed to get the patio bed level and firm. If the patio is fairly large it's sensible to get your friendly neighborhood bulldozer operator to level it off quickly. (Put the sods upside down in the compost heap and add the topsoil to your raised beds.) Try to preserve a slight slope—about ¼ inch to the foot—

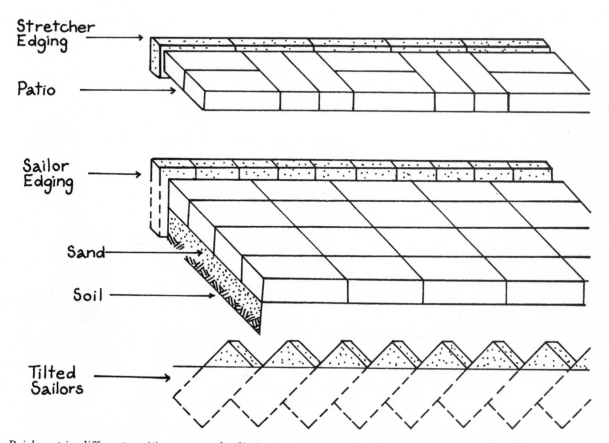

Stretcher Edging

Patio

Sailor Edging

Sand

Soil

Tilted Sailors

Bricks set in different positions can make distinctive edgings that give different architectural moods to a walk or patio or flower bed border.

so water won't stand and collect below the surface when the patio is done.

Lay out the patio outline with stakes and mason's twine, getting the corners at perfect right angles. Be sure that the size of the patio will fit the brick pattern you're using so that you come out even with bricks and space—it's depressing to have to go down to the brickyard again for 13 more bricks, or to have to cut dozens of bricks to odd sizes to fit into the patio layout. Go over the entire earth surface with a tamper—a length of 4 x 4 will do very well—and compact the soil to avoid hollows and pits.

Setting the Edging

After laying out the patio carefully and getting it square, lay the edging carefully, to guidelines. Edging is the most tedious and most important part of the job. Two good types of edging, useful also for beds and borders, are made up of either a level row of sailors side by side or soldiers set closely together. Plain sailors standing in a row are economical, quick to set in, and strong. An old favorite bed-edging variant is tilted sailors to make the dramatic saw-toothed edge. This edging is often seen around old-fashioned perennial borders, and

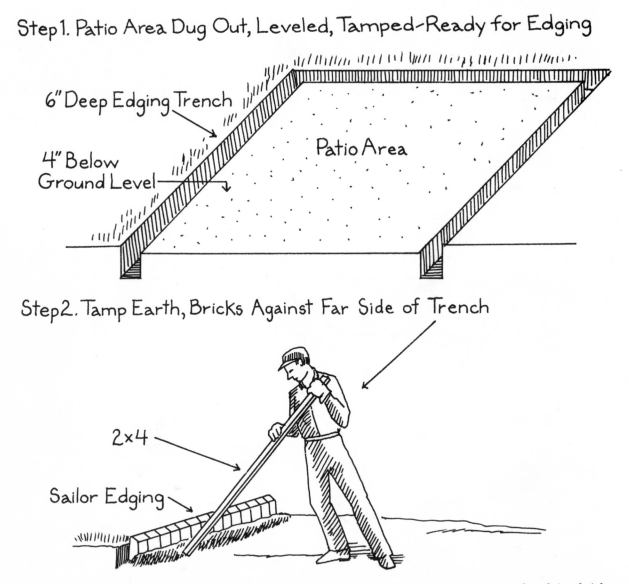

Step 1. Patio Area Dug Out, Leveled, Tamped—Ready for Edging

6" Deep Edging Trench

4" Below Ground Level

Patio Area

Step 2. Tamp Earth, Bricks Against Far Side of Trench

2x4

Sailor Edging

Doing the ground work for a dry-laid brick patio is the most vital part of the job. As soon as the edging bricks are set and tamped into place, the invisible patio can be clearly seen in the gardener's mind. Careful measuring and good choice of the brick pattern are important; the bricks should fit the space without a final row of odd-sized or odd-shaped bricks that must be custom cut.

while some gardeners find the undulating effect quite fetching, it has always looked to me like a stegosaurus rising out of the earth. The sharp corners of bricks arranged this way can be a potential hazard if someone should fall on them; therefore a tilted sailor border is *not* recommended for patio edging. Preservative-treated 2 x 4s are used by some gardeners as short-cut edging, but they won't last as long as brick, and replacing them will be a headache a few decades from now.

1. Around the perimeter of the level patio area dig an edging trench 6 inches deep, depending on whether the edging will be flush with the patio (safest), or will project slightly above grade. A sharp trowel may be a better tool for this job than a shovel. Try to keep the sides of the edging trench straight up and down.

2. Set the bricks in place snugly and evenly. Tamp the soil against their inner edges so that they are firmly butted against the outside wall of the trench. A short piece of 2 x 4 makes a handy tamper here. When the edging is completed you are ready to prepare the sand bed.

Building the Sand Bed

A level bed of damp sand 2 inches deep makes a firm but flexible cushion for the bricks.

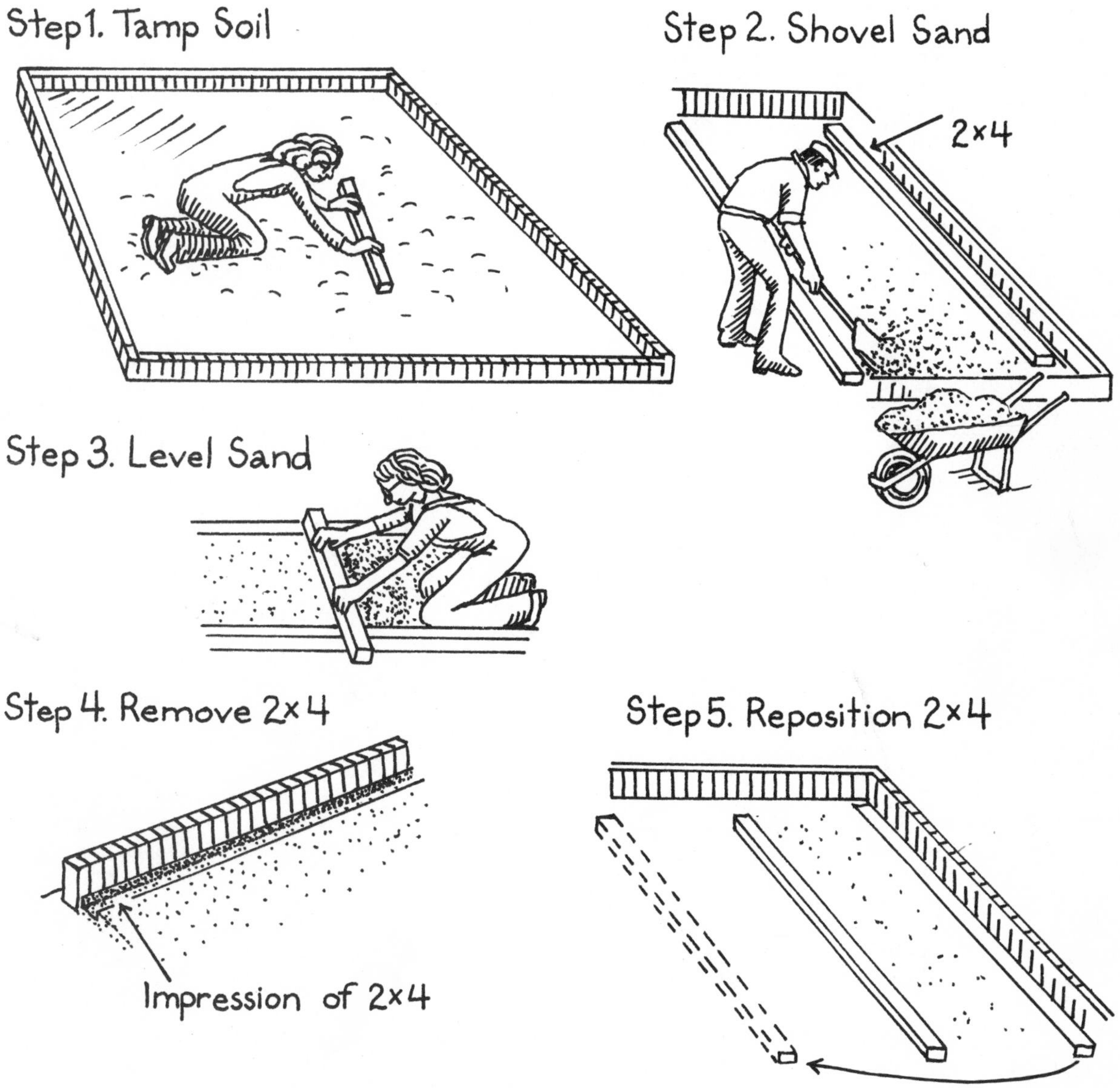

Step 1. Tamp Soil

Step 2. Shovel Sand

2×4

Step 3. Level Sand

Step 4. Remove 2×4

Impression of 2×4

Step 5. Reposition 2×4

The secret of leveling a bed of sand is to work on a small section at a time.

1. Before dumping on the sand, tamp down the earth again, or roll it until the soil surface is firm. If the patio area is large, you may get tired of your 4 x 4 tamper. You can rent powered tamping tools from local equipment rental suppliers. Work from one side of the edging to the other, back and forth.

2. Set one 2 x 4 flat against one edge of the patio perimeter and another 2 x 4 3 or 4 feet away and parallel with the edge. These are temporary edgings that make it easy to level the sand with a screed in convenient sections. Shovel the damp sand, misted with the hose an hour earlier, into the first section, trying to distribute it evenly.

3. Use a 2 x 4 as a screed. Rest it across the temporary 2 x 4 edgings, then drag it toward you over the sand to level it.

4. Remove the 2 x 4 abutting the patio edging and fill in the cavity level with sand.

5. Set the free 2 x 4 parallel with and 3 to 4 feet beyond the 2 x 4 already in place to form

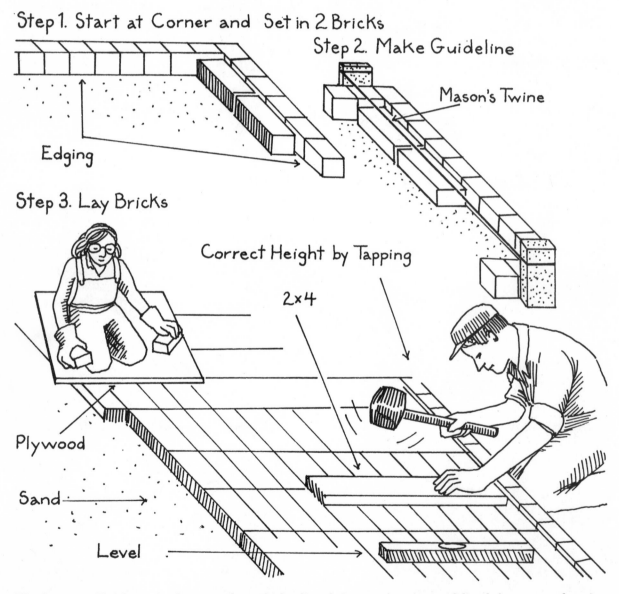

The first row of bricks set in place must be perfectly aligned. A mason's twine guideline helps you set them in position with a minimum of error. Distribute your weight over the still unsteady bricks by working on a piece of old plywood.

another parallel alley ready to receive sand. Shovel in the sand, level it with your 2 x 4 screed, remove the old 2 x 4 temporary edging and continue until the entire patio area is filled with damp and leveled sand.

Laying the Brick

It's a good idea, no matter what pattern you are laying, to set up a guideline for the first course of bricks so you don't inadvertently work in an off-kilter angle.

1. Before you set the guideline, start at one corner and set in two bricks.
2. As shown in the illustration, tie each end of a length of mason's twine around an upright brick and set these bricks outside the patio edging at each end of the patio to make a taut, straight line exactly one brick's width from the edging. Use this as a guide for the important first course.
3. Lay the bricks tightly together following your chosen pattern, cutting bricks where it is necessary. You can work from one edge toward the other, so that you are always on the new-laid brick and never disturb the leveled sand. To keep from dislodging the new-laid bricks, lay a piece of plywood over them before you kneel or put weight on them. Gardener's knee pads are a wonderful help at this stage of bricklaying.

Check the surface often with a level. High and low spots mean rain puddles and frost damage. Level the bricks by laying a short length of 2 x 4 over them and tapping them down level with a hammer. Continue in this fashion until the patio is laid.

Filling the Cracks

Fine sand is what holds the bricks of the patio together. The coarse sand used for the bed won't do. You can sift coarse sand through screening to get the fine variety, or you can buy several bags of special fine sand already sifted. However you get it, pour it onto your new brick patio and work it diagonally down into the interstices between the bricks with a stiff-bristled push broom. You will have to do this several times for a few weeks until the cracks are filled up and the bricks locked together.

Working fine sand down into the cracks between the bricks with a push broom will lock each brick into place.

Flagstone Patio

A flagstone patio can be set in sand even more easily than brick, for the weight and mass of the stones means no edging is necessary. Special paving flagstones can be bought in varying thicknesses, but for setting in a sand bed, those about 2 inches thick are best.

To figure out how much flagstone to order, compute the square feet of the patio area and tack on 10 percent for trimming and waste. Flagstone is sold by the square foot.

Prepare the area and the sand bed just as you would for a brick patio.

Set in the flagstones. Flagstones are irregular in shape; if you want a snug fit—¼- to ½-inch space between the stones—you will have to do some stone trimming. *Always put on a pair of safety goggles and gloves before you chip or trim stone.*

If you have worked with the thicker, rougher fieldstone in dry wall building, you will find shaping flagstones similar but easier. Chip away sections of stone gradually with a stone hammer or a point and hammer until the stone is the right shape. A smart blow directly on the place where you want it to break usually ends badly with the break in quite the wrong spot. Because flagstone is fairly thin, sometimes it's

Scoring a Stone

Sand

Breaking a Stone

Safety Goggles

Board

possible to use this method of shaping it: set the stone in the sand and score along the desired break line with a cold chisel and hammer, then set the stone on a board so that the unwanted section is suspended past the edge of the board; finally, strike the stone a number of moderate blows on the unwanted side until it breaks, one hopes along the score line. You might have to score both sides if the stone is resistant to this manipulation. Fight any urge to give the thing a great whanging smack.

After the stones are all in place, fill in between the cracks with fine sand several times over a period of weeks.

When cutting any kind of stone, protect your eyes with safety goggles. Scoring flagstone and breaking it to shape is easier than working with fieldstone, but the chances for injury are still there.

CHAPTER 8 _____

BRICK AND FLAGSTONE WALKS

Hundreds of thousands of gardens and yards have been made beautiful and traversable with brick and flagstone walks. Garden walkways mean clean feet, pleasant daily walk-throughs even in rainy weather, easy wheelbarrowing, and easy moving about of Rototillers, cultivators, lawnmowers and garden carts.

Garden walks should be planned with two objects in mind—good accessibility to the beds, and good drainage. You can set side alleys of stepping stones off the main arteries of garden walks to make every part of the garden simple to get at.

Brick walkways should always be built on a gentle slope if possible so that rain and melt water can run off. A low or flat walkway in the garden means standing water injurious to plant roots.

Both brick and flagstone walks can be set into sand beds or even directly into sandy soil. A brick path should be treated as a long, narrow patio in the building process, and must be set with sturdy edging to hold the bricks in place and keep them from shifting around under foot traffic. It is not amusing to stumble on a loose brick when you're carrying a bushel of ripe tomatoes to the kitchen.

Flat fieldstone or cut flagstone walks should be made up of the largest stones you can handle. The smaller the stone, the more likely it is to get dislodged or shifted under a garden stroll-

er's weight. Set the stones as close together as possible and fill in the gaps with sand. Even so, once a year you will have to patrol your walks, rooting out dandelions and crabgrass that have

managed to get a foothold in the tiny cracks that separate the stones.

Herb gardeners like a walkway with beds of fragrant low-growing herbs such as the thymes or camomile lining the path. Sometimes these aromatics are encouraged to grow in the spaces between the flagstones so that anyone walking along the path will be enveloped in the rich scent of the leaves crushed underfoot. Mother-of-thyme *(Thymus serpyllum)* and lemon thyme *(Thymus xcitriodorus)* are particularly pleasant. A special turf brick with a hole in the center is made for just this treatment. If you intend to plant herbs between the bricks or flagstones, fill the joints with fine soil instead of sand.

Innumerable gardeners have set a brick or flagstone walk directly into the soil without a bed of sand. Each stone or brick has to be custom-seated, and there is a great deal of scraping, hollowing, digging, and trial and error to get the pavers secure and level so that they do not wobble. After a season or two such walks tilt and subside in places, but they are still traversable by the wary, and a really troublesome brick or stone can be reset easily.

The Gravel Path

Gravel paths are inexpensive and versatile in woodland gardens and in plant sanctuaries, preserves and parks. They can be made broad and spacious enough for several people to stroll along abreast without sending you to the poorhouse, and they give excellent traction underfoot. They can traverse slopes and grades with railroad tie steps acting as miniature retaining walls (see Appendices, "Railroad Ties"). They also blend harmoniously with almost any garden or landscape.

There are nevertheless some disadvantages to gravel paths. They must be edged to keep the gravel from getting into beds or lawns. Weeds will spring up and must be rooted out. Every few years the gravel will have to be replaced or augmented. Sandal-clad persons will curse your gravel walks for the inevitably painful bits of gravel that work up under their toes. Bird and wildlife watchers are not overly fond of gravel paths, for the scrunch-scrunch of every footstep warns the shy pippet and the wary woodchuck that a threatening human is approaching.

If you decide on gravel paths, keep them away from your vegetable garden. Even with edging, the gravel spreads everywhere, and it is extremely difficult to move garden machinery along a gravel path.

1. Always edge a gravel path with brick or cut stone. There is a special dark green plastic edging made for exactly this purpose available at most garden centers and in discount store handyman departments. It looks terrible—like dark green plastic—unless you set it abutting a lawn and as deeply as you can and still contain the gravel. Preservative-treated wood makes a good but expensive edging if the path is a long one. Railroad ties set along the edge of a gravel path work well but give the walkway a heavy, overbearing character that suggests you are walking toward one of the seven wonders of the world.

2. One inch of pea stone gravel spread evenly and directly on the smoothed and leveled ground makes a decent path. A deeper layer will have strollers slipping and wading in gravel as they toil along. Bank-run gravel—the kind used on country roads—contains clay particles which swell when they are wet. A path of this gravel will eventually pack down into a hard, smooth walkway that is very pleasant in mild weather, but muddy in rain and dusty in drought.

CHAPTER 9

BRICK WALLS

Although versatile bricks can be laid comfortably on the ground with only sand to hold them together, when you begin stacking them up into walls mortar is needed to secure them. Brick steps without mortar can be dangerous, since they have neither the weight nor mass to hold them in place. If you live where good flat stones for a dry wall are scarce or expensive, brick makes a fine, mellow garden wall.

A low brick wall less than 3 feet in height usually will not need a building permit, but it's better to be safe than sorry. Most communities have increasingly complex and detailed building codes that can affect everything from a wall to a walk.

Bricklaying Basics

If this is your first try with bricks and mortar, pick a simple project for your first one or until you get the hang of laying bricks.

Bricks for use with mortar are *nominal* bricks; their measurements include space for the standard ½-inch mortar joint, so a common nominal brick will actually measure 7½ inches by 3½ inches by 2¼ inches. Anyone who has done time cleaning mortar off bricks knows all about this. The mortar filling in place makes up the vertical and horizontal *joints*.

A low wall 2 or 3 feet high is usually two bricks wide. A strong, popular and good-looking way to lay bricks into a wall is plain old common bond, a combination of header and stretcher courses. Stretcher courses are rows of bricks laid longways to the foundation. Header courses, so called because all the bricks are laid with their heads out, are similar in form and function to the bind stones in a dry wall; they tie the brick wall together.

Common bond is four stretcher courses, one header course, another four courses of stretchers, one more header and so on to the top of the wall. The wall is capped, usually with a row of headers turned on their narrow edges. In this position they are called *rowlocks*. The basics of bricklaying are applicable to all the bonds shown on page 68, and if you've worked with kindergarten blocks in your youth you have enough experience to build a wall using any of these bond patterns.

Bricklaying is full of curious and ancient language, but a few basic techniques explained will get the gardener where he or she is going without studying vocabulary lists at night.

Holding a Mason's Trowel Hold the trowel much as you would a kitchen pot full of gravy which you intend to pour into a gravy boat—your thumb on top and your palm up under the handle. This is a labor-saving hold: to distribute the mortar along the bricks evenly—called "throwing a line"—the hand turns the loaded trowel in an easy, fluid motion, 67

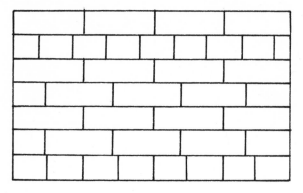

Common Bond

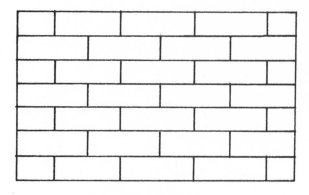

Running Bond

English Bond

Flemish Bond

Popular bond patterns.

and moves along three bricks. This is an acquired skill—if you can spend a short time by the side of a skilled brick mason taking a lesson or two in the technique you will save yourself hours of awkward effort. You might think on the early Virginia settlers—aristocrats unused to hard labor—who, to get the necessary shelters built, were pushed by Captain John Smith into the vigorous wielding of axes to trim logs for houses. Strong language accompanied the labor, and it was ordered that for every oath muttered or shouted, the speaker should have a can of water poured down his sleeve at the end of the day. Many of the unwilling and unaccustomed workers had sodden sleeves at nightfall.

Spreading the Mortar After the mortar line is thrown along three bricks, it has to be spread out evenly with the point of the trowel to make the horizontal joints. Ideally, no glob of mortar should ooze out over the side of a brick under the weight of the brick that is shoved

onto it. Accidents do happen, however; if the mortar does slop over, use the trowel to cut off the excess, and use the excess to butter the next brick.

Buttering the Bricks Before each fresh brick is set down into the freshly spread mortar, it must be buttered with mortar itself on the end that will butt up against the preceding brick. This makes the vertical joints.

Building a Free-Standing Garden Wall

A low brick wall or any other mortared brick structure needs a poured concrete footing because the superstructure must stay level and rigid or the mortar will crack, break and fall out of the joints. The concrete footing takes a good bit of digging and a fair amount of gravel and concrete, either mixed by you or fetched by the concrete truck all ready to pour.

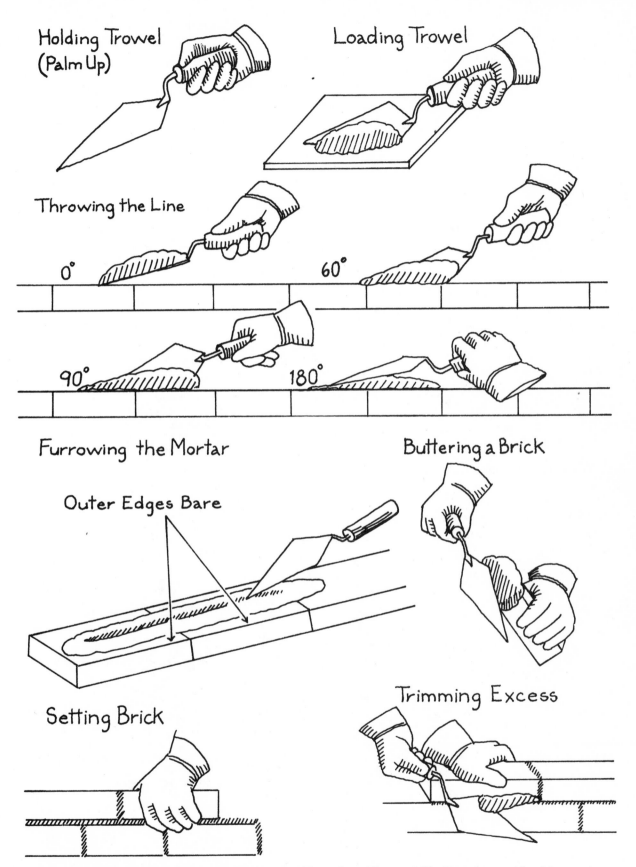

Holding Trowel (Palm Up)

Loading Trowel

Throwing the Line

0° 60° 90° 180°

Furrowing the Mortar

Outer Edges Bare

Buttering a Brick

Setting Brick

Trimming Excess

Learning to throw a line and to butter bricks smoothly and rapidly are skills that take considerable practice. Follow the procedure shown, working slowly, until you get the feel of it.

Mark Lines for Trench

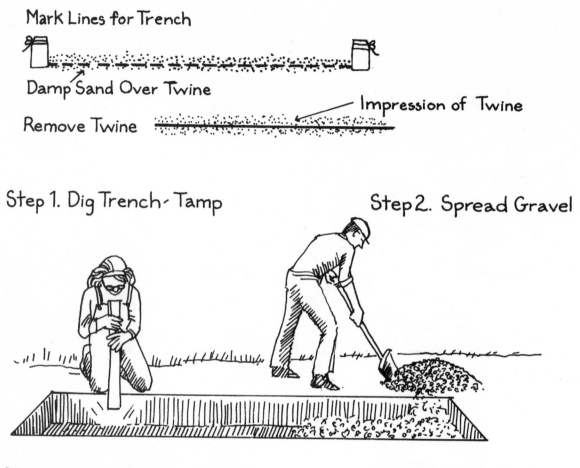

Damp Sand Over Twine

Impression of Twine

Remove Twine

Step 1. Dig Trench - Tamp

Step 2. Spread Gravel

Step 3. Pour Concrete - Level

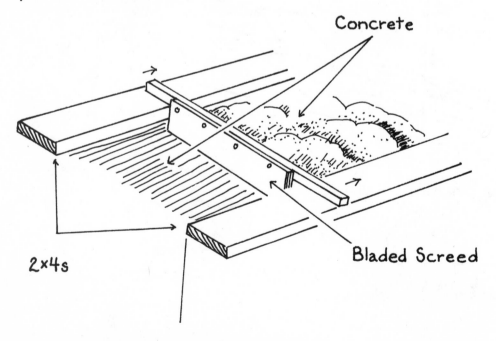

Concrete

2×4s

Bladed Screed

Pouring a concrete footing to support a brick wall is necessary if you want the wall to stand for a while. The project is easier if your shovel is sharp, and you have help.

The Concrete Footing

Mark lines on the ground for the trench where the wall footing will go. A clever trick to keep your shovel free from entangling strings is to set a taut cord (the mason's twine again) at ground level along the line, then sprinkle it with enough sand to cover it lightly. Mist the sand until it's damp, then lift the string straight up and there is a ruler-straight trench line in the sand.

How deep and wide to make the trench? A rule of thumb for footings under brick walls says the footing should be as deep as the wall will be wide, and the footing should be twice as wide as the wall. Our two-brick-wide wall occupies 8 inches of width. This, then should be the depth of the footing, which in turn rests on 6 inches of gravel. If we follow the builders'

rules, the footing will be 16 inches wide with the wall running down the center as if it were on a platform. However, our low brick wall need not have such a wide footing. It can do nicely with a 12-inch-wide concrete footing. The trench then will be 14 inches deep and 12 inches wide. The footing should be 2 inches longer at each end than the wall itself will be.

If your soil is firm enough to hold a vertical edge, you need not bother with footing forms or edge forms.

1. Dig the trench and get the bottom as level as possible, then tamp it well with a 4 x 4.

2. Spread 4 to 6 inches of gravel in the bottom of the trench. All footings need a gravel base for good drainage.

Edge Forms for a Footing

If your soil is crumbly or if the upper edge of the trench is broken and loose, you will have to build some edge forms so the footing comes out level and plumb. Because concrete is very heavy it can bend and warp flimsy forms, so brace the edge forms well. Use scrap lumber for this project.

1. To avoid disturbing the soil of the trench sides any more than necessary, lay the edge forms out flat on the ground at the precise dis-

tance they will be set in the trench and nail in the spreaders.

2. Set the edge forms in the upper part of the trench. You may have to do a little more gentle digging with a trowel to get them level and straight.

3. Drive 2 x 2 stakes into the ground outside the edge forms to hold them secure.

4. Pour the concrete. Level it with a screed. Let the footing cure three or four days before you remove the forms.

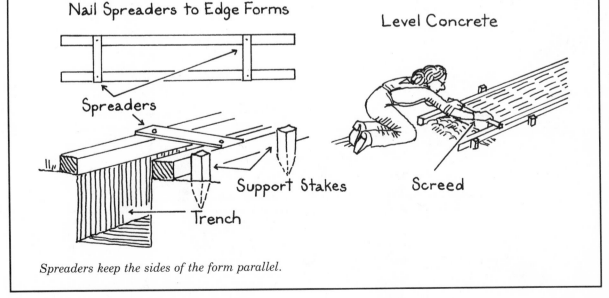

Nail Spreaders to Edge Forms

Spreaders

Support Stakes

Trench

Level Concrete

Screed

Spreaders keep the sides of the form parallel.

3. See Appendices, "Cement—The Heart of Concrete and Mortar," for directions on mixing your own. Pour in the concrete until its surface is about ¾ inch below ground level. If you used edge forms, you can screed the concrete level, but if you have only the earth sides of the trench for a form, you can either gently tamp the concrete level with a section of board, a hammer and a level, or lay two level 2 x 4s on the ground at each side of the trench, make a screed with a blade as illustrated on page 70, and draw it over the concrete to level it.

4. Let the concrete cure slowly for four or five days. Cover the surface with a sheet of plastic, far superior to the old damp burlap sacks once used for curing. If you do use burlap sacks, they must be sprayed several times a day to keep them damp as the footing sets.

Putting Up the Wall

You need: bricks, mortar, a trowel, a carpenter's pencil, a chalk line, a brick set, a hammer, and of course the inevitable ball of mason's twine and blocks.

The bricks are all delivered, the footing in place and well cured, the mortar mixed and the trowel at the ready. You are ready to lay bricks. Because the footing is wider and slightly longer than the intended wall, you must mark the wall's outline on the footing. Use a snap chalk line to mark this outer line.

The Dry Run To come out even without cutting any bricks or getting involved in higher mathematics, a dry run is important and will save you many headaches.

1. Lay out dry courses of stretcher bricks along your chalk lines. Ideally there should be ½ inch of space between bricks but if this means the bricks won't come out even, it's better to adjust the spacing than to cut the bricks.

2. On the edge of the footing surface, mark with a carpenter's pencil the placement of each brick. This is your guide to getting the all-important first course right. Remove the dry-run bricks from the footing.

Laying Up the Leads Forty-five minutes or so before you start laying the bricks, hose the brick pile down with water and let it stand until the surface wetness evaporates. The bricks should not be dry and thirsty when they're laid, for they will absorb the water in the mortar mix and weaken the chemical bond.

1. Throw a line of mortar three bricks long inside the chalk line mark for the course. Lay the first brick by pushing it downward and toward the end of the footing until it is aligned with the pencil marks for brick placement. Check with a level.

2. Butter the end of the next brick that will butt up against the first brick. Lay it in

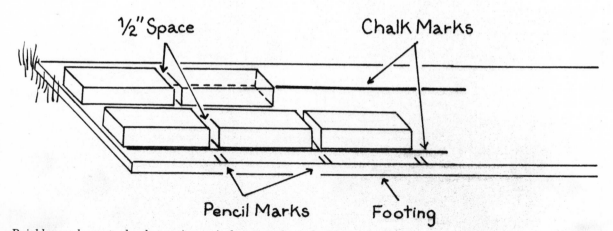

Dry Run

½" Space   Chalk Marks

Pencil Marks   Footing

Bricklayers learn to develop patience. A dry run takes a little time but can save you from hair-tearing errors.

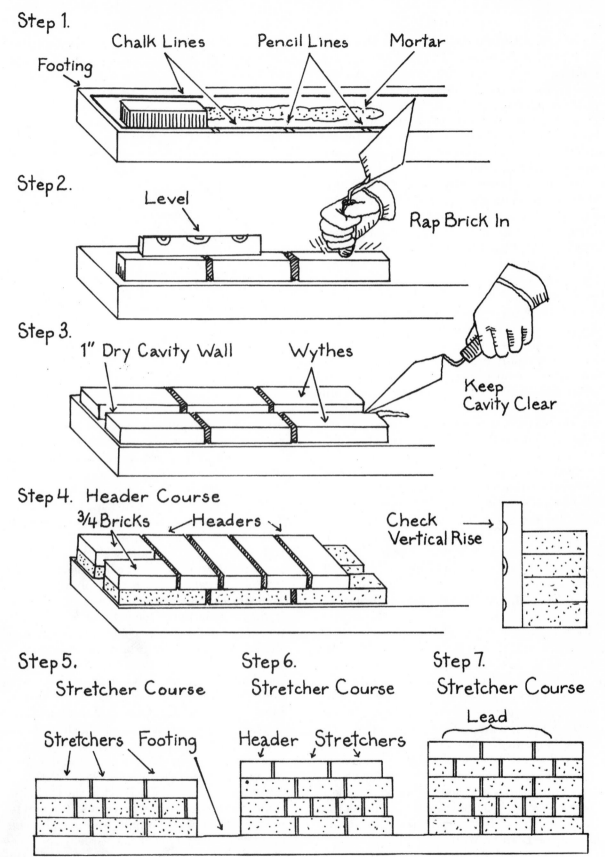

Step 1.

Footing Chalk Lines Pencil Lines Mortar

Step 2.

Level Rap Brick In

Step 3.

1" Dry Cavity Wall Wythes Keep Cavity Clear

Step 4. Header Course

¾ Bricks Headers Check Vertical Rise

Step 5.
Stretcher Course

Stretchers Footing

Step 6.
Stretcher Course

Header Stretchers

Step 7.
Stretcher Course

Lead

A brick wall rises at each end before the middle is filled in. Laying up the leads is like building a three-dimensional interlocking puzzle, and is absorbing work.

place as you did the first brick. Do the same with brick number three. Check with a level to see whether the bricks are level. You can use your trowel handle to rap the bricks level. Don't pick up and reset a brick that has been laid— it breaks the rapidly forming chemical bond between mortar and brick. If you must reset a brick, remove the mortar and discard it, then butter the brick anew.

3. Instead of working down the length of the wall as you did when you laid out the dry run, go to the other side and lay the first three bricks of the backup course just as you did on the near side. These two parallel rows of bricks are called *wythes,* and are actually two side-by-side narrow brick walls. The 1 inch of space between them is *not* mortared, for this is what is called a dry cavity wall. Were the two wythes linked with mortar, moisture could seep in and build up in these inside joints, then freeze, expand, and finally disintegrate. The dry cavity wall allows moisture to run down the inside walls and out. Try not to let globs of mortar fall into the cavity as you work, for each lump of mortar is a potential sponge for moisture. Large brick buildings are often built with cavity walls.

Don't worry that the wall will be weak without an interior mortar bond; the header courses in the common bond design will tie the wall together strongly. (However, if you decide to build a wall in running bond, you will have no headers to bind the wythes together. In this case, metal wall ties should be laid every 12 inches on each even-numbered course.)

4. Although there are only six bricks of your wall in place, the next step is the second course, or header course. Walls of brick are built from both ends toward the middle. Building up the ends is called the *lead,* and it is generally five courses high. To start this course off right, cut four bricks to ¾ size and set two aside to use at the other end. Now lay the ¾ bricks parallel with the first course at the end of each wythe, then lay the headers.

5. The third course of the lead is a simple stretcher course. Remember to keep the bricks level both on the line and across the wythes. As the lead rises, check the vertical line of the wall to be sure it isn't turning into a local version of the Leaning Wall.

6. The fourth course is a stretcher course also, but it commences with a header so the

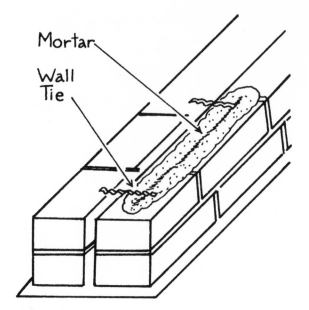

The wythes of a wall built in running bond must be tied together with metal wall ties.

bricks will fall one-on-two, two-on-one, with never a joint directly over another.

7. The fifth course is a straight stretcher course. Keep checking vertical alignment. At this traditional point you have finished one lead as brick workers have been doing for centuries. Repeat the procedure exactly on the other end of the footing. When both leads are finished, it's time to fill in the blank space between them.

Filling In Here's where beginners run into trouble, largely because they plunge ahead, laying brick madly, anxious to see the wall rise. If the wall is fairly long, there is a natural tendency for a sag to get built into the middle. Professional bricklayers always work with a guide—a taut line of mason's twine level with the top edges of the bricks in the course being laid. The line should be about ¹⁄₁₆ inch away from the bricks. Amateur brick workers have a tendency to set their bricks flush with the line, and before the course is run these too-close bricks have pushed the line out and distorted the entire row. Bricklayer's argot for this is "crowding the line." Bricklaying savants have written treatises on the proper use of the line, but the gardener who only wants a pleasant brick wall around his or her garden should remember that the line is simply a guide for the eye, not a rigid mark for precision placement

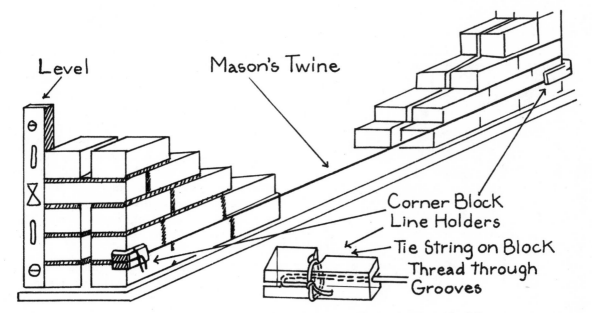

Level

Mason's Twine

Corner Block
Line Holders
Tie String on Block
Thread through
Grooves

A guideline of taut mason's twine keeps the courses level and reduces the chances of building in a center sag.

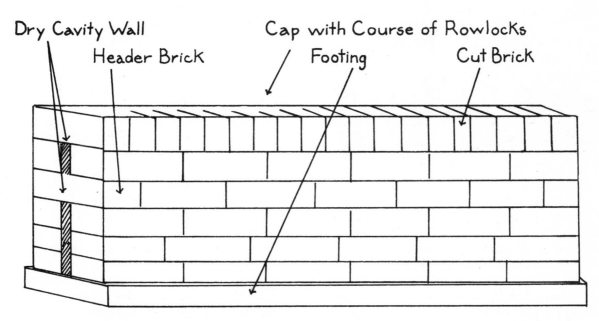

Dry Cavity Wall
Header Brick

Cap with Course of Rowlocks
Footing

Cut Brick

Capping the wall gives the project a smooth, finished appearance. Any uneven cut brick should be buried in the row rather than stuck on the end where it will be more obvious.

of bricks. A ball of mason's twine (used in nearly every project in this book) usually comes with two corner blocks made to attach to each end of the lead at the level the bricklayer wants. This simple arrangement saves much time and trouble.

The Second Lead Finally you have built up the wall so it is level with the leads. The last brick is buttered (on both ends) and dropped into place. What now? If you want the wall to go higher, you simply begin all over again. Imagine the top level of the course you have
(continued on page 78)

Special Project   The Raised Herb Bed

Older gardeners who have trouble bending over and stooping appreciate the comfort of raised beds. A small but tall herb bed outside the kitchen door in a sunny spot can hold four or five of the household's favorite culinary herbs and be easily tended. Sometimes a tiny raised garden—useful, very easy to care for and set off handsomely in its brick bed—can light a glow of enthusiasm in people who are ill, infirm, depressed or just feeling bored and useless. A few hours of your labor, some bricks and mortar, a wheelbarrow of good soil and compost and a few plants can make a great difference in another's enjoyment of life. It's a better present than a box of candy or cut hot-house flowers on a remembrance day.

A 2-foot-square structure 32 inches high will give nearly 4 square feet of planting room—enough to fit in parsley, chives, thyme, basil and dill—all at near waist level.

The project will take about 120 bricks, a trowel, shovel, carpenter's pencil, 4 square feet of flat paving stones or concrete paving blocks for the foundation, a wheelbarrow of sand and several bags of ready-mix mortar. Coreless concrete paving blocks only a few inches thick are available at most building supply stores. They're inexpensive and work well in this project.

1. Mark the outlines of the raised bed on the ground and dig out the foundation about 4½ inches deep, or enough to allow a 2-inch bed of sand and a foundation of paving block or stone. The foundation level should be ½ inch or so below ground level.
2. Put in the sand, level it, then set in the foundation blocks. Fill the cracks with fine sand.
3. Lay out a dry run of bricks for the first course as you would for a brick wall and mark their positions on the foundation with the carpenter's pencil.
4. Have the mortar ready and proceed to lay the bricks as you would for a wall, but here, because the bed will be filled with soil supporting growing plants, drainage is extremely important. By omitting the step of buttering the ends of the bricks *for the first course only,* you will build in weep holes that give excellent drainage.
5. Unlike the free-standing wall, the brick bed has corners. Study the illustration and note the overlap position of alternating courses of brick. Build up the structure, course by course, checking with the level to keep the bricks even. Because the structure is small, you needn't bother with a guide line, but set a 2 x 4 across the courses frequently—a level atop the 2 x 4 will tell you what you want to know.
6. Cap the bed with a row of rowlocks or bricks in any posture you like. Let the mortar cure for three or four days before you fill the bed with compost and loamy topsoil.

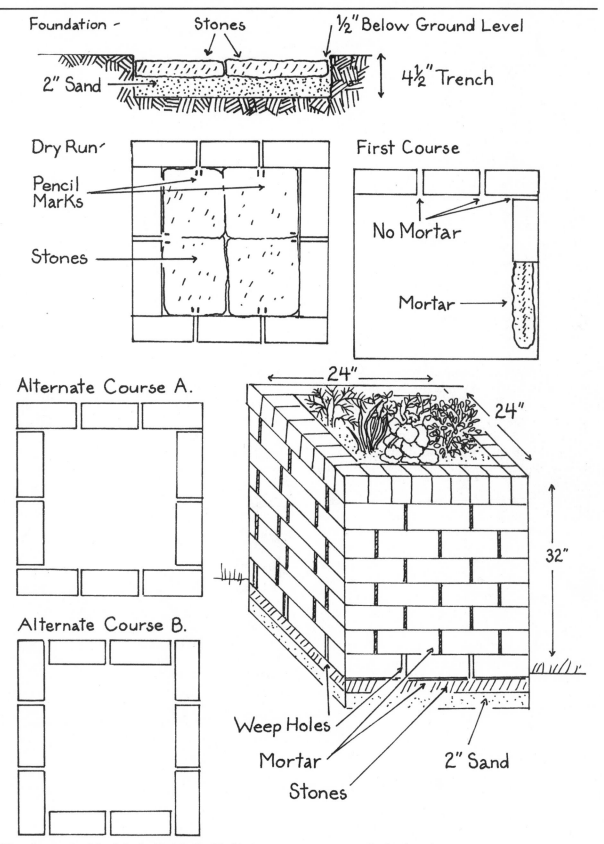

Foundation -
Stones
½" Below Ground Level
2" Sand
4½" Trench

Dry Run
Pencil Marks
Stones

First Course
No Mortar
Mortar

Alternate Course A.

Alternate Course B.

24"
24"
32"

Weep Holes
Mortar
Stones
2" Sand

Plan for a raised herb bed of brick. Build this in a sunny spot near the kitchen door.

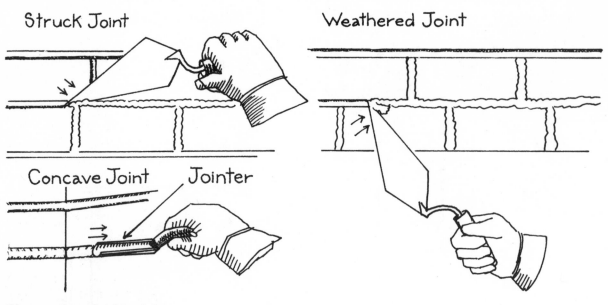

Three common finishing joints.

just finished is the footing, and once more build up leads at both ends, precisely as you did in the beginning. Then fill in the middle. Keep checking levels and alignments and work with the line as a guide. Every once in a while, narrow your eyes and sight down the wall—this is the best way to pick up sways, low spots and humps.

Finishing Off The classical cap for a common bond wall is a course of rowlocks along the top, but you can cap it as you like. If you have to cut a brick to finish the row, try to discover the need before you reach the end. That way you can bury the cut brick in the row where its odd size won't be so noticeable to the public eye.

Every hour or so as you work on your wall, you should finish off the mortar joints. Excess lumps and globs of mortar you will have cut off with the edge of the trowel as you built each course, but the joints must be smoothed and slightly indented. Special mason's tools called *jointers* are used to make concave or beveled impressions along the mortared joints. The smooth surface and the angle protect the mortar from weathering. You can also use the point

of your trowel to strike the joints—that's one reason trowels are pointed.

The best time to strike the joints is after the mortar has started to set and is firm but still slightly plastic in consistency. Do the long, horizontal joints first, then the vertical joints. With the edge of the trowel sweep away any crumbs and bits of mortar squeezed out by striking the joints. The final touch is sweeping down the wall with a good broom or a dry scrubbing brush after the joint mortar has set.

Experiment to Suit Your Own Place

In the garden, bricks, footings and your new skill can be combined to build brick benches with wooden slatted tops, sheltered niches along a wall for tender plants, plant containers and raised beds within the interior of a patio, low retaining walls, sturdy edgings, walkways and paths. You can also construct a brick-paved ramp from the toolhouse to ground level to eliminate wrestling lawnmowers and tillers up and down steps as they are put in and taken out.

3
WALLS
and Other Stone Constructions

CHAPTER 10 _____

STONE WALLS— REMINDERS OF A FLINTY PAST

New England is stone wall country. At the turn of the century much of New England was farmland and hill pasture; there is little left now of that fallen farmers' civilization except the stone walls in the somber woods, enameled black by early spring rain, and the carefully laid corners of cellar walls filling slowly with drifted leaves and the dark scent of earth mold. Although the region's bucolic, Jeffersonian age is long gone, the tessellated landscape is still divided by thousands of miles of stone walls that hem old cemeteries, mark forgotten boundaries and line roads no longer travelled, for they were built to last by men who never dreamed that beech woods would rise again on their wheat fields and sheep pastures.

Lichens grow on the ancient stones like opened fans, whorled lace circles and ash pale islands and archipelagos traced on stony maps. The walls are pierced by countless crevices and black interstices where mice, beetles, snakes, spiders and chipmunks live; woodchucks burrow underneath, their vaulted halls crowned with stone ceilings that eventually collapse in silent disaster, pulling down a section of hard-built wall. Carelessly thrown-up walls laid haphazardly on the earth have long since fallen into rubble heaps, tossed by the annual tides of spring frost heaves. Uncapped walls have lost their upper stones to the crashing limbs and deadfalls of winter storms. Even the best and strongest walls split apart and tumble into chaos

from the relentless thrust of a growing tree. The walls have been there a long time, but they will not stand forever.

Unmended and untended, the stone work of the past is disappearing—mark of New England's stony soil, evidence of obdurate toil and index of rock-ribbed character, of faces as expressionless as stones, of a kind of blunt, stonelike humor, exemplified by the old New Hampshire fellow who was clearing a field by building a wall 4 feet wide but only 3 feet high. An outlander goggled at it and inquired why it was such a peculiar shape. The New Hampshirite continued to fling the rocks into place, but said clearly, "So's if the wind blows 'er over, then she'll be taller than she was."

There was a sound reason for that broad wall. Walls that rimmed very stony land were sometimes built as two carefully constructed parallel walls—the so-called double wall—with a generous distance of several feet between them, and the storage alley in the center was filled with the round and odd-sized stones, dumped in any way they happened to fall. The finished wall was capped with large flat stones that served as roof and stabilizer. Such walls were very broad, low, and rarely blew over.

A Crop of Stones

Stones were New England's best crop, drawn from deep below the earth to the surface by the *81* relentless twisting and wringing of the frost, and the plow. From the view of the farmer who had to harvest the rupestrian crop, there were three kinds of rock: flat rocks which could be fitted together easily to make a strong, well-knit stone wall, the awkwardly shaped and un-handy fieldstones which were exasperating to work with and made a precarious wall in any but the most skillful hands, and the impossible round and football shapes that ended in the rubble pile.

Most walls were a mixture of flat stones and fieldstones. Uncountable numbers of stones went into the miles and miles of dry walls, stronger and more flexible than any mortared wall would be in a climate where the earth heaves and subsides in freeze and thaw; and still the stones kept coming, generation after generation.

Most stone was found in field and furrow ready to use, but farmers were skillful with stone hammers, wedges and shims when they discovered a good supply of mica schist rock ledge, and split off from the handy farm stone quarry beautiful flat slabs for doorsteps, walk-ways, hearths, springhouse floors, chimneys, root cellars, and tidy walls around the garden.

The Morality of Walls

In early days there were two compelling motives for building stone walls—to clear the

---

Harvesting Stones

Daniel L. Cady, "popular poet of rural life," was a Vermonter who practiced law in New York but amused himself by writing dialect poems about life back on the farm. Although they barely escape being doggerel, most of the poems have the granite grain of a harsh rural life in them. Here is an example from *Rhymes of Vermont Rural Life* (Tuttle Company, Rutland, Vermont.)

"Picking Stone" in Vermont

There's nothing quite so lorn and lone
In rural life as "picking stone";
It holds the record 'round the farm
For making farmer boys "disarm";
It's sent more help off "down below"
Than milking, chores or shoveling snow;
It's made more hired men decamp
Than too much souse or too much samp:
No sadder stunt was ever known
Around the farm than "picking stone."

Each year when we begun to cart
The grain, a sickness hit my heart;
I knew that through them fields I'd go
Again in 'bout a week or so;
I therefore rubbered far and near
To see if "stone" was thick that year;
I tried the stubble with my shoe
To see if it would puncture through—
Oh! I can always spare a moan
When I remember "picking stone."

Anon, some hot September day,
When puppies felt too warm to play,
And geese was too het up to hiss,
I'd get directions 'bout like this:

"This afternoon I spect to 'tend
That auction down at Greensboro Bend;
You best put on your old brogans
And after dinner lay your plans,
When I'm away with neighbor Sloan,
To try your hand at 'picking stone.'"

And so I tried—both hands I tried,
Both feet and every part beside;
I pawed and clawed and poked and kicked
And toed and heeled and purled and picked;
Each hand a bar, each foot a skid,
I pried like gamblers on a "lid,"
The puffballs filled my eyes with smoke,
My fingers bled, my back was broke,
The thistles scratched my crazy bone—
I wished that I could turn to "stone."

My face was camouflaged with dirt,
But still 'twas whiter than my shirt;
Each time I kicked a cobble free
About a hundred bugs I'd see,
A hundred kinds of wigs and worms
And microbe spawn and cocoon germs;
I'd heave the cobble on the pile
As though I'd 'scaped from something vile—
Alas! the thoughts have never flown
That grew in me when "picking stone."

But what such farming had to do
With getting rich I never knew;
A funny crop—the more the yield
The less the listers taxed your field;
The more you raised, 'twas strange to tell,
The less you had to eat or sell;
It made my farming faith so weak
That off I went to study Greek,
And back I've come to make it known
That Adam's curse is "picking stone."

fields of rock, and to fence off gardens, crop fields and pastures from the depredations of livestock. Later, other reasons made good sense to New Englanders; picking, hauling, piling stones and building stone walls was work to be done in any slack time, for idle hands were the devil's tools; so there came to be a kind of moral righteousness built into a stone wall. Then, too, the endurance of the structures made them proper for boundary lines, maintained by the neighbors who shared the wall, during a day of common work in the spring after the frost was out of the ground. One of Robert Frost's best-known poems, with its pervasive sense of tradition in the reiterated line "Good fences make good neighbors," is *Mending Wall* from the 1914 collection, *North of Boston.*

Good gardeners prized stone walls on the north and west sides of their gardens, for the stones absorbed heat during the sunny days and gently radiated it out at night, broke the force of wind and weather moving in from the west, and, when placed at the back of a south slope, offered some protection from the first cold autumn frosts rolling down the hill.

Mysterious Stones

The people who own grown-over New England farms today are often from urban or suburban backgrounds, coming back to the land. To them, the subsiding, collapsing walls are picturesque ruins, more attractive in their nostalgic evocation of the past than useful as boundaries or fences. When fences are wanted, they are ugly and expensive barbed wire or electric strands strung along the broken backbone of neglected stone walls, even though a week's labor could mend the gaps and restore the wall to beauty and utility. The stones are free, already gathered and hauled to the site; a little rummaging in the leaves turns them up. Mending a wall is the best way to learn how to build one. There are other rewards than a repaired wall, a new skill and a sense of accomplishment for wall menders: sometimes cider jugs and old bottles, leaned against the shady side of a wall during haying time long ago and then forgotten, are found half-buried in the leaves.

Modern ignorance of the skilled Yankee stone work of past centuries has produced some strange ideas. In recent decades a number of sensationalist articles in the popular press claimed that the stone chambers built into Ver-

mont hillsides were ancient Celtic and Phoenician sanctuaries and temples. It took a scholarly study by Vermont State Archeologist Giovanna Neudorfer to snuff out these bizarre theories and restore credence in the homely root cellars built by great-great-grandfather to store his turnips.

Old Walls

In the seventeenth century every New England town had its *fence viewer,* a person with the unusual occupation of travelling about and checking that fences and walls were the proper height. Stone walls were usually about 4 feet high, but some three-footers were topped with a single high rail to bring them up. Stones, especially the large, flat slabs, were valuable in early days and none went to waste. Watertown, Massachusetts, had to go so far in 1677 as to legislate how long a person who dug up a stone in the highway, but did not immediately remove it, might claim that object as his own.

Not all stone walls surrounded farm fields. The country houses of the eighteenth century rich sometimes had very fine stone walls 6 to 8 feet high, set with elaborate gates. Around Portsmouth, Rhode Island, some of the finest stone walls in the country are still standing after 300 years. Howard S. Russell, in his richly documented history of farming, *A Long, Deep Furrow,* comments that in Rhode Island and the adjacent corner of Massachusetts, many stone walls were built with unwilling Indian labor.

> If the Indians did not work according to their contract, they were "summarily flagallated." When during the Revolution, Dartmouth (today part of New Bedford) was raided by the British, one Indian inhabitant at least regarded it as a deliverance. "I make no more stone wall for Joseph Russell," he chalked on his employer's barn door, before going over to the enemy.

Stone quarries developed in many towns that were rich in schists, phyllites, limestones or gneisses, all of which have obvious foliation planes that make them easy to split with hand tools, and a few places regulated the sale of stone. Some men were better and faster at building stone walls than others, and skilled dry wall masons, adept at setting sturdy foundations, constructing sound corners and devising cantilevered stone stile steps, followed dry walling as a trade. Stone builders from Cornwall, Wales or Scotland were outstanding wallers in a land of stone workers. Often a local man particularly good with stones would hire out in his slack periods of farm work, and build stone walls for others at a price, sometimes on contract, sometimes by neighborly verbal agreement. Wall was usually paid for by the rod, and old accounts list such contracts.

An interesting note by Alice S. Whitney of Wilmington, Vermont, gives us an idea of building rate and pay rate in the last century for wall work. "About 100 rods of our north property line dividing two farms was built by grandfather Zenas Whitney for 16 cents a rod. The stone wall is still standing and is truly high. He averaged four rods a day." This was a tremendous speed in stone wall building—one rod is 16½ feet, generally considered a good day's work for two men!

The Garden Wall

In colonial days many gardens had a stone wall on the north, and fence around the other sides. As livestock moved off the common and into private, fenced fields, the garden wall became rarer. Although the walled garden is one of mankind's most ancient and beautiful structures, it never enchanted Americans as it did people in more crowded parts of the world, where gardens were private retreats with pleached walks and beds of exotics hidden behind walls like secret jewels in locked cases. Inside these gardens the walls were used as backdrops for intricate espaliers or fine grapevines. The walls calmed wind, muted noise and shut away the sight of the marketplace and the traffic on the road.

But in this country there was too much land, too much room, too much wild space to bother walling in a garden, and our cultural taste for the open, unenclosed plot and the flat open lawn was set rigid. Now, when we are more and more closely crowded, our eyes assaulted by our neighbor's plastic flamingo or by squat, striding power transmission towers, or our ears stressed by the whine and snarl of traffic, there is a considerable need in our lives for the serenity of the walled garden, the "inland island" Swinburne described in *A Forsaken Garden* when he wrote:

In a coign of the cliff between lowland and highland,
At the sea-down's edge between windward and lee,
Walled round with rocks as an inland island,
The ghost of a garden fronts the sea.

Stones still speak to some of us. Poet and stone worker Robinson Jeffers sheltered his sea coast garden behind high, mortared stone walls that took him many years to build. Wall building is a good occupation for a poet, for as he or she turns the stones and considers their shapes, the same may be done with words until the one that fits is found.

Types of Stone Walls

"Throwed-up" Walls In the days of building with stone there were several kinds of dry walls. The more common "throwed-up" walls found along country roads and around cultivated fields were laid directly on the earth, the largest and levelest stones making a sturdy base. The smaller stones above overlapped and fitted together by the stone mason's rule of one-on-two, two-on-one. At intervals these smaller stones were fixed in place by big tie stones, also called bind stones. Two men working with a team of oxen and a stoneboat averaged about a rod a day of throwed-up wall. The work was easier on level ground. On steep or rough terrain, or when the stones had to be hauled a long distance, the work was much slower, maybe only 6 or 8 feet a day. The practice was to haul stone to the site over a period of months before the work of laying up stone commenced.

Churchyard Walls Another sort of stone wall, usually built around the cattle yard outside the barn, around the garden or graveyard, orchard or church, had a deliberate, sober dignity, and was painstakingly constructed for permanence with meticulous craftsmanship. Before a single stone was laid, a trench was dug down to the sub-soil, sometimes down below the frost line. Then the big foundation stones were set level and true at the bottom of the trench with gaps between to allow drainage. The wall was built up carefully, one-on-two, two-on-one, tie stones every few yards, a slight batter or taper built into the sides to shed water, and a barely perceptible V-shaped trough that ran the spine of the wall from bottom foundation stone to cap stone so that the downward pull of gravity would bind the wall structurally over the centuries.

It took great skill to recognize the correct position for each individual stone in the wall to maintain the sidewall batter and the V-trough depression, as well as to keep all surfaces true and level. Only the finest and flattest stones were used in these beautiful walls. The weight of the rock was evenly distributed, and gaps were chinked with small flat or wedge-shaped stones. The wedges were set with the leading edges pointing either toward the interior of the wall or toward the face, according to local preference, and there was great controversy (and still is) about the merits of "chinking out" versus those of "chinking in."

Large, flat stones were saved for the cap stones that finished off the top of the wall. Walls taller than 4 feet were often double walls, bound together with frequent tie stones. The ground at the base of these walls was sloped away to give good drainage, a relatively simple job done by packing the earth from the preliminary excavation in a slope along the finished wall.

Conscientious farmers chose to build even their field walls in a method that fell between the "throwed-up" wall and the elegant churchyard wall, with a dug trench and a good foundation, but using fieldstone as it came in the upper wall. In *A Book of Country Things*, Walter Needham described wall building in his grandfather's day to author Barrows Mussey:

They would plow the loam where the wall was going, and shovel it out more or less to the subsoil. Then they would draw the stoneboat along beside this trench, and roll the big ones in for foundation stones. Quite often they would wall off a ten-acre lot, forty rods one way and forty rods the other. Sometimes it was only haphazard.

After Gramp had rolled the big stones off into the ditch, and set them to suit him, he would draw the boat beside of it. As fast as the boat come along he would take off the small stones that a man could pick up, and he'd place them right on the wall, and build it straight ahead just as easy as you please. He worked so fast you might have thought he was just throwing them in at random, yet when he got through, the wall was as solid as if it was one rock.

For most of us, building a stone wall is a slow, careful art: it takes much practice to develop an eye for choosing and placing stones, much strength to wrestle and roll the larger stones to their places, and much patience to fit the stones together correctly. A dry wall is like a three-dimensional jigsaw puzzle with awkward, monstrous pieces, and the solution is not so much found as made. But there are very few occupations that give such extraordinary satisfaction, and fewer that will endure so long. When you build a stone wall well it will stand for centuries, outlasting almost everything else you may do with your life.

Oddly enough, very little has been written about the way to construct a dry wall, perhaps because, as one stone mason says, "The only way to learn to fit stone is to do it."

CHAPTER 11

BUILDING STONE WALLS

Are you in good physical shape? If you're a gardener, you're used to stooping, bending, hoeing and digging, but stones are heavy, obdurate objects and wall building means a great deal of lifting, heaving and prying. The work will slim down your waistline and build your biceps, but it's easy to overdo things in the zeal of adding just one more stone before daylight fails, or trying to move too large a rock by sheer effort. You can hurt yourself seriously.

Before You Move a Stone

If you spend most of your time sitting at a desk, if you are not used to physical labor, or if you are overweight, have back problems or any kind of heart difficulties, talk with your doctor before you start building a stone wall.

The most common injury in stone work seems to be back injury. If you pick up a stone, even a small one, while bending over, you can hurt your back in several ways. Never pick up heavy weights while your spine is curved—squat down and lift with your legs.

Cuts, bruises and mashed fingers are also pretty common in a crowd of stone workers. Wear heavy gloves with rough surfaces while working with stone. Rough leather gloves are the best; cotton wears out in a few hours, and it does not give you a good grip. When you put stones in place, never set them down—inevitably setting stones in place means squashed, pinched fingers. Instead, drop each stone into its bed. Watch an old hand building a wall and you'll see that he drops and even flings the stones into place. This technique also seats the stones more solidly, and gives a satisfying, final sound to the building process, like the old Vermonter who would heave a big one onto the wall with a heavy thwack, then remark with satisfaction, "*that* one ain't goin' nowhere!"

Stout work shoes, preferably with steel toe caps, are the only kind of footwear to use when wall building. The fool who goes wearing sneakers or sandals to the stone pile can suffer injury that will keep him or her hobbling for weeks.

If you plan to chip and trim away protrusions and wobbles from rocks, to shape rock, or split it, a pair of good safety glasses is essential. Flying stone splinters can partially or totally blind you.

Quarrying stone and dynamiting ledge rock are extremely dangerous activities unless you've been trained and know what you're doing; even then insurance companies that will take you as a risk are hard to find. Even the careless use of a crowbar in a stone quarry can bring down tons of killer rock square on top of you. Leave quarrying and dynamiting to the experts, or you may not be able to finish your stone-work project at all.

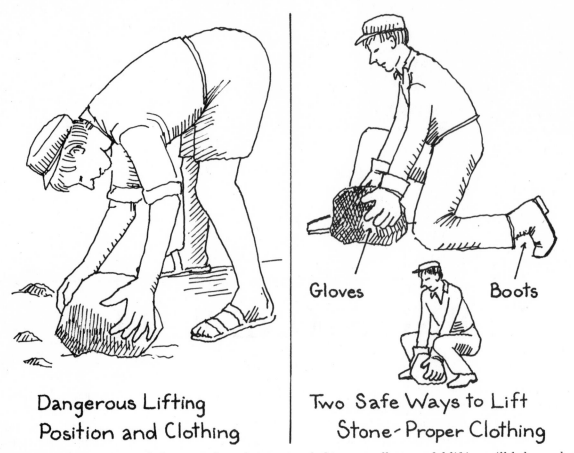

Dangerous Lifting
Position and Clothing

Two Safe Ways to Lift
Stone - Proper Clothing

Gloves   Boots

Building with stone is rough, heavy work, and protective clothing as well as careful lifting will help you last longer.

Forget any kind of stone work on a wet day. Wet stones are slippery and treacherous, both underfoot and in the hand. Wait until they're good and dry before you start handling them. If a long spell of rainy weather sets in, curb your impatience; the stones will still be there when the rain stops, and so will you.

Building a wall necessarily means a handy pile of stones that you've collected and hauled to the work site. Clambering around on the pile looking for the right stone can be pretty risky; it's easy to lose your balance on loose stones and go sprawling onto some of the hardest surfaces and sharpest corners you've ever felt. Keep the work area tidy—it's a nasty experience to trip over the sledge hammer or a stone that's been set aside for later placement when you're carrying a big one to put on the wall and cannot see your feet or obstacles on the ground.

Finally, don't try to lift and move huge stones by brute strength, for you'll wear your-

self out in a week if you don't rupture or strain yourself. Humans are engineers; use some of the tricks with inclined planes, levers and rollers described in the section "Moving Big Stones" later in this chapter to get the monsters into place with a minimum of risk.

Tools for Stone Work

The kind of stone you use and the project you work on both determine the tools you need. A fieldstone dry wall can be laid down with only a few essential tools like a stone hammer, a level and a crowbar, but precision-shaped stones in some elaborate stone work may demand specialized sculptor's tools like bush hammers and toothed chisels. These tools are too fine and delicate for ordinary stone work.

Stone workers develop individual styles that affect their choice of tools; one person may insist on careful placement of natural rock forms

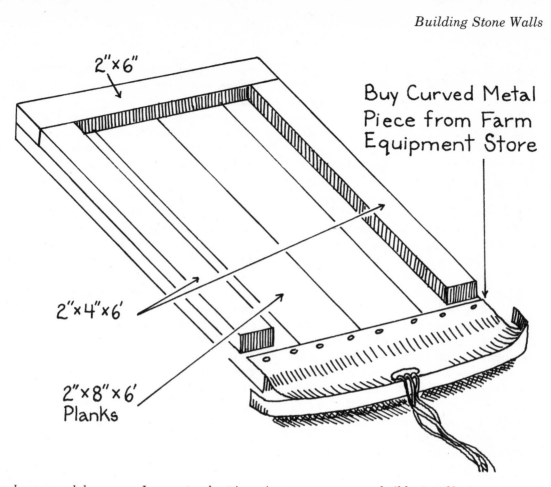

2"×6"

Buy Curved Metal
Piece from Farm
Equipment Store

2"×4"×6'

2"×8"×6'
Planks

If you have a work horse or a Jeep, a stoneboat is a nice accessory you can build yourself.

and be willing to spend an entire day searching for just the right rock to fit a space, while another will spend just as much time chipping, tapping and shaping a non-conformist rock until it fits.

Getting the rocks and stones to the site of the project is the biggest part of the job. In the old days, suitable fieldstone was piled in an out-of-the-way corner all during the year, then dragged to building sites at slack times; a stoneboat and a team of work horses, the farmer and the hired man made up the vehicle and the motivating power. Stoneboats are still to be found at country auctions, and they can be built fairly easily if you want to make your own. But a stoneboat is not much good unless you have something to pull it. Work horses are making a slow return to the rural world, and if you have a team or if your neighbor does, you can snake rocks out of places where motorized vehicles can never go. Without a horse you need a Jeep or other rugged 4WD vehicle to pull the stoneboat—it's definitely not a family project. If you

don't have a horse or the vehicle, your ability to gather quantities of stone from your own field and furrow is limited, and you don't need a stoneboat.

A garden cart with large wheels can be used for carrying a few smaller stones over fairly level ground, but if these carts are loaded heavily with stone the axles will give way or the wheels collapse. *Stone is very heavy.* It doesn't take many rocks to make a ton.

The wheelbarrow is the devil's invention when it comes to moving rock. It's difficult to roll up even a slight incline when loaded with heavy stone, and maddeningly easy to tip over if the load is not perfectly balanced. Just the same, a wheelbarrow is a good deal better than carrying stones one by one in your arms.

If you've got stone piles on your land—or somewhere else—you can hire a truck to bring the stone and dump it on your work site; you may have to load them on yourself.

Spade A sharp digging spade to prepare trenches, to level soil and to dig out rocks is essential. Don't use the spade as a lever to raise big stones from their beds; this is why crowbars were invented, to save spade handles. Keep the spade sharpened.

Crowbar This wonderful tool is invaluable for prying up rocks, turning them over, moving them along, loosening them from their beds in the soil and levering partially split layers apart. You can still pick up crowbars at country auctions for a few dollars. An old crowbar should get a bright coat of paint, for the dull dark iron makes the thing disappear right before your eyes when it lies on the earth or in a litter of leaves.

Gad-Pry Bar This excellent little tool, developed for hobby rock hounds, is very useful if you have schist or layered stone you want to split. It has two hammering faces that give it a double function, both as a point chisel and as a pry. You hammer the point into a rock seam by pounding on point A with a crack or mash hammer, then lever the layers apart without using another tool or re-siting the gad-pry, by hammering against point B.

Pinch Bar Many stone workers find a short pinch bar useful in prying and levering rocks. Others will have a pinch bar lying handy for six months and never pick it up once.

Hoe-Pick Another of those multi-use tools, the hoe-pick can pry up rocks, dig with the pick end, level off with the hoe end or wedge its way in between stubborn stones.

Stone Hammer This is the tool you'll have in your hand most often when building a wall. The stone hammer has two faces, one flat and one beveled. You can both split rock and shape rock with a stone hammer. It's handy to have two weights—a four-pounder and the little one-and-a-half pounder.

Crack or Mash Hammer Bearing two flat or hammering faces, the crack hammer is designed to be used with points or cold chisels. Short handles and heads of 3 or 4 pounds make the crack hammer very useful. You should not use your stone hammers to drive chisels, but pick up the crack hammer instead.

Sledge Hammer An 8- or 10-pound sledge with a long handle has plenty of uses when you're working stone. You can break a rock apart, drive wedges into the seams of layered rocks or set a misplaced stone into position with a sledge. The very heavy 25-pound sledge recommended by some stone workers is useful only if you quarry or split giant slabs of rock from

a ledge. Half an hour of swinging this monster leaves your arms feeling like stretched rubber bands.

Geologist's Rock Hammer These are often listed as desirable tools for beginning stone workers. Don't waste your money. They are light and delicate tools, best used to pick out small samples of rock and do a little light shaping. You can build a hundred-foot fieldstone wall and never pick up this hammer once.

Bush Hammer Looking very much like a meat tenderizer, the bush hammer is only for delicate, fine shaping work on soft stone such as sandstone, limestone and marble. The same is true for the **Toothed Chisel**. Both of these belong more in the sculptor's studio than on the stone mason's rock pile.

Chisels If you are going to shape rock or split it, you need chisels. With these tools you can work most rock surfaces from lumpy distorted wobblers into flat, useful structural objects.

Point Chisel A tremendously useful tool often called simply a "point." It channels the energy of a hammer blow into its relatively narrow point, and the burst of power against the stone surface, repeated over and over, eventually breaks off or chips away the offending knob. A point is the only way to make an impression on the hard, small-grained types of stone such as granite.

Cold Chisel Also called a **Common Chisel**, this tool has a broad cutting end that distributes the energy of a blow along a wider line than a point. With many types of stone the cold chisel can strike away respectable chips from the surface, but its major use is in splitting rocks along a seam.

Both kinds of chisel should be used with a crack hammer, not a stone hammer. Chisels should be sharpened frequently, not to the fine edge of a woodworking tool which would crumple and fold under with the first blow against stone, but to relatively thin wedge. Many stone workers keep a handful of chisels nearby since they dull up quickly with use.

Wedges If you are splitting rock along its seams, several old axe heads make fine wedges. You start the crack with the cold chisel, then drive in the axe heads with the crack hammer or the sledge until the stone splits or the crack widens enough to admit the point of the crowbar.

Rollers Six or eight short lengths of 2-inch iron pipe, about 2 feet long each, are indispen-

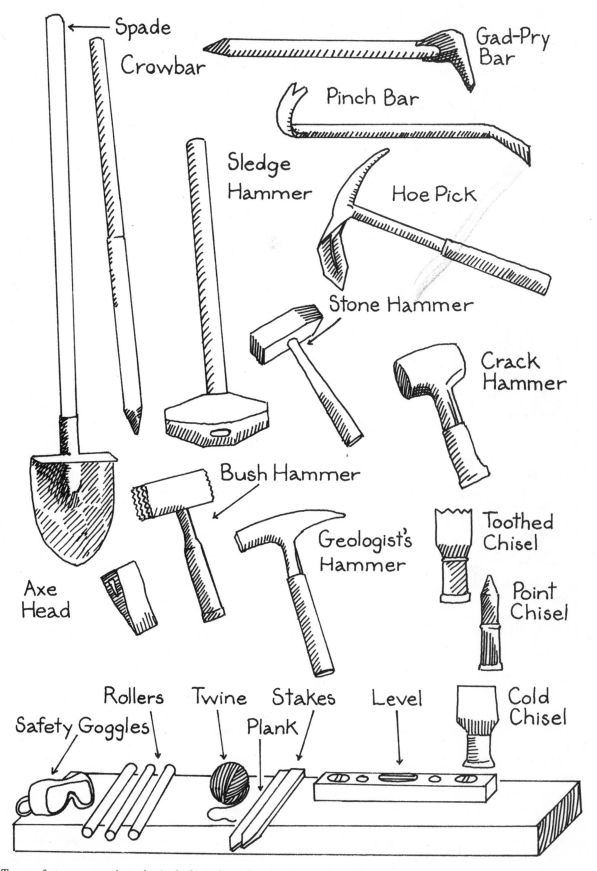

Spade

Crowbar

Gad-Pry Bar

Pinch Bar

Sledge Hammer

Hoe Pick

Stone Hammer

Crack Hammer

Bush Hammer

Axe Head

Geologist's Hammer

Toothed Chisel

Point Chisel

Rollers Twine Stakes Level Cold Chisel

Safety Goggles Plank

Types of stone mason's tools, including those for shaping and positioning stones.

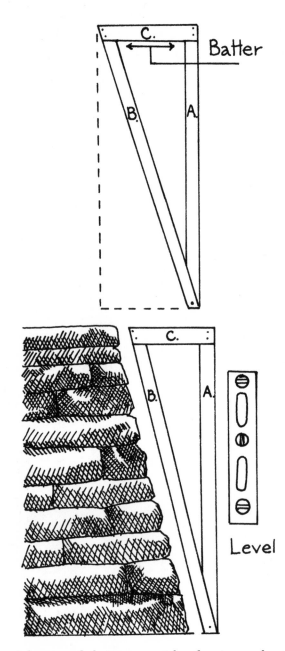

A home-made batter gauge takes the guesswork out of tapering a wall.

the stone wall inward as the height rises; it's much superior to guessing.

Level, Stakes and Ball of Twine These tools are important for laying out the line of the wall and keeping the structure level and straight while you're building it. If you're planning on building a curved wall, use the gardener's trick of laying out the pattern with a flexible garden hose, the way curving perennial borders and shaped beds are marked.

What Kind of Stone Have You Got?

Not many of us want to take a course in geology before we start to build with stones. Half an hour of handling the rocks from your property or environs, tapping them with a point, or trying to chip an edge or to split them with the stone hammer will show you what you've got in terms of physical properties. If you're working with fieldstone, you'll select rocks for their natural shapes and spend little time cracking, hammering and shaping. If you're fortunate enough to have a nice supply of metamorphic rock with good cleavage planes like the hard shales and schists that are plentiful in the Northeast, you can split and shape slabs with relative ease. Almost impossible to shape with hand tools are the extremely hard granites and other plutonic rocks, but their hardness doesn't bother the fieldstone wall builder if he finds good shapes. Unfortunately, many granite rocks are baroque in shape.

Where to Find Stone

Old foundations or walls—on your property or elsewhere with the owner's permission—are wonderful sources of building stone if they are in awkward, non-useful places or in severe disrepair. Rather than let them disappear into the ground, rebuild them in more advantageous locations. They have been pre-sorted and assembled in one area for you. All you have to do is get them from where they are to where you want them.

Streambeds are not good places to take stone from, despite the advice of some stone masonry books. Several states prohibit the removal of stones, gravel or sand from streams and rivers, for doing so, even on a small scale, can change the contours, the shapes of the pools, even the

sable in moving big rocks along a plank to the wall.

Planks For wall building, an assortment of sturdy 2-inch-thick planks in different lengths and widths are essential. These become inclines and bridges over which you transport stones too heavy to lift by turning them over and over, or by rolling them along on your pipe rollers.

Batter Gauge A homemade instrument, the batter gauge tells you how much to taper

flood levels along the waterway. The consequences of this tampering may not be noticeable for years, but it can, in the end, have a deleterious effect on the health of the stream.

You can patiently gather stones from your bean patch or gardens, from plowed fields, from banks along the side of the road where maintenance crews have pitched rocks and boulders for years and from the property of neighbors and friends, but this slow accumulation can take many months or even years. If you enjoy working with stone, however, let this casual accumulation become a habit; you can never have too many stones.

It is almost a sure thing that somewhere in your county or state there are old mines or gravel pits. These places are usually remarkably well stocked with interesting stones and rocks, just lying there for the taking if the mines are closed down. To find such rock sources, buy the topographical maps for your area; sporting goods shops specializing in hunting and fishing

equipment usually carry a number of adjoining maps for the surrounding region. The symbol for an open pit or quarry is a tiny pick and rock hammer with crossed handles in black. The town clerk can give you directions to the quarries. Once there, restrict yourself to loose stone; do not start quarrying stone yourself—it is dangerous and illegal unless you have the owners' permission.

Another excellent source of rock and stone can be found in the Yellow Pages of your telephone book under *Quarries*. Rock quarries often have grout piles of scrap and waste stone they will sell very cheaply or even give away. Often, though, the grout piles contain huge slabs of rock weighing a ton or more each. The quarry foreman can tell you whether there is a local stone shed where you can get smaller, more or less squared-off slabs and chunks of rock of easily handled size. Such stone can be delivered locally for very reasonable prices. If you have your own truck you can pick the stone up your-

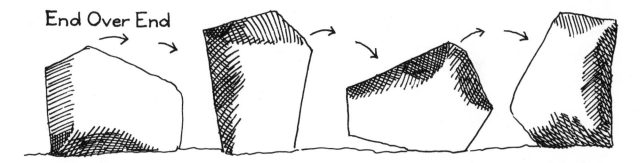

Rolling Stones

Levers, rollers and inclined planes make it possible for a puny human to move enormous, weighty rocks.

self for just about nothing. The advantage of getting a large pile of rocks together at once is to allow you to start on the project right away without spending months accumulating stone.

If you live in a section of the country where stone is scarce and expensive, it may make more sense for you to build a fence. Or you might arrange to make your next vacation a trip to a major quarry region in a sturdy truck. The benefits a stone wall can confer on a garden (storing warmth from the sun, protecting plants from early wintry winds) make it worth a great deal of trouble to get enough rock to build such a wall.

Moving Big Stones

Getting big stones from the woods or remote fields down to your stone pile is a job for the horse and stoneboat, or the Jeep and logging chain. But some big stones that are not too far away from your project can be moved, with persistence, by rolling them end over end, as shown on page 93.

Rolling Stones End over End You can move a stone a long way by tipping it up on one end, pushing it over, tipping it up again, and so on. It's slow but effective. Use the same technique to get big rocks from your stone pile

Step 1. Mark and Brace Stone   Step 2. Strike Bevel-edged Sledge

Step 3. Set Axe Head in Crack

Brace Stones

Step 4. Pry Apart with Crowbar

Splitting stone is hard but satisfying work. Most beginning stone workers are thrilled with this mastery over an apparently obdurate and unbreakable substance.

to the project. If you want to move the stone up onto a wall, make a ramp with stout boards—double boards if the stone is very heavy—and support the planks underneath with wood rounds or stacked stones. Keep on flipping the stone end over end, but *very carefully* and slowly.

Rolling Stones on Pipe Rollers Use your crowbar and a leverage stone to work the obdurate giant onto pipe rollers arranged on the inclined planks. Push the stone up the ramp carefully with the crowbar, setting each roller freed by this movement in front of the stone until you reach the top. Jimmy the stone into place with pry bars. A truly behemoth rock can be moved more easily, according to stone mason Curtis P. Fields in his little book, *The Forgotten Art of Building a Wall,* if it rests atop a short plank over the rollers.

Splitting Large Stones

There it is, a great fat chunk of schist weighing hundreds of pounds, perfect for several doorsteps, a couple of hearth stones, or a good section of your garden walkway—if you can split it in two. You can, if you have two sledge hammers (one with a beveled edge), and someone to help you.

1. Turn the stone on its edge so that the cleavage planes are clear to see and easy to approach. Mark a chalk line where you want the rock to split along the cleavage planes. Brace the stone with smaller stones for support so that it can't fall over while you're working it.

2. Set the beveled splitting edge of one sledge on the line near the center of the stone. Have your helper strike the flat surface with the other sledge. Repeat this action many times near both ends of the slab and in the center until a crack begins to show.

3. Using an old axe head as a wedge, set the blade in the crack near the center with your crack hammer, then hammer the head in with the sledge hammer as far as it will go—this may only be an inch or two. Two axe-head wedges are better than one. The axe-head wedges will rarely split the slab, but will open up the crack enough to let you force in the point of your crowbar.

4. Insert the crowbar as far as possible, and begin working the crack open with leverage—back and forth, back and forth. At length, with a peculiar dry sound, the slab will split through in a clean, smooth break.

Splitting a smaller stone. Always seek out the natural cleavage lines and work on the point of least resistance.

Splitting Small Stones

Smaller chunks of schist or other striated rock with good cleavage planes can be split by setting the beveled edge of the stone hammer along the desired split line and striking the flat side of its head with the crack hammer. You may need to use the cold chisel to get the split started.

Patience is the primary force in splitting rock. No rock is going to snap apart like a billet of dry birch.

Shaping Stone

Put on your safety glasses before you pick up a hammer. For beginners there are limits to shaping stone, but wall builders usually find it enough to crack off protuberances that make unsteady wobblers of decent rocks, to chip away an end or side so that a stone will fit into a certain place, or to break off an awkward corner. It is amazingly easy to have a stone break in the wrong place after you've been patiently working on it for 45 minutes. A sudden sharp blow on the desired break line tends to make the stone break somewhere else. A slow and steady method of chipping away at a corner far from the objective and gradually creeping up on it with a patient tap-tap-tap gives the best results. The flat faces of your stone hammers

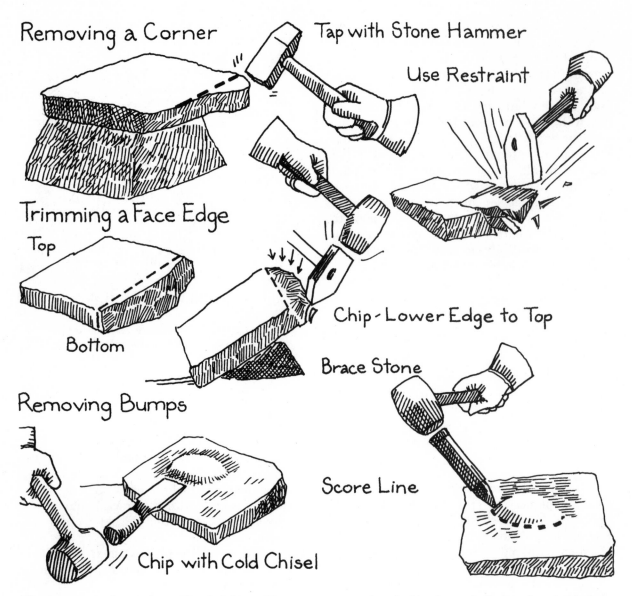

Removing a Corner

Tap with Stone Hammer

Use Restraint

Trimming a Face Edge

Top

Bottom

Chip – Lower Edge to Top

Brace Stone

Removing Bumps

Score Line

Chip with Cold Chisel

Shaping stone takes patience. Hurried, heavy blows mean assorted rock chips instead of trim, shapely blocks.

are the usual surfaces for chipping and shaping rock, but the chisel and crack hammer used together do similar nibbling of hard stone.

Removing a Corner

1. Set the rock with the unwanted corner on another rock, letting a small part of the corner in question extend into space. (Some stone workers prefer laying the stone in a bed of sand.)

2. Tap the corner tip with the flat or "cutting" face of the stone hammer, chipping off small bits and pieces and getting the feel of the individual stone's resistance and fracture qual-

ities. Each stone will behave differently under stress.

3. As the corner gradually disappears under your carefully controlled assault, move the rock forward into the sphere of action.

Resist any impulse to give the thing a great hearty whack and have done with it—this sends razor-sharp splinters of stone flying and usually breaks the stone in the wrong place. Take heart in the knowledge that corner removal is a skill that is slowly learned, and that as you work the corners off more and more stones, you'll become fast and proficient.

Trimming a Face Edge

1. Begin by drawing a line to show what should be whittled away.

2. Set the stone up on a few rocks at an angle suitable for comfortable work; you'll be here a while.

3. Set the beveled edge of the stone hammer at an angle of about 30° near the bottom of the unwanted section. Chip away small pieces of stone by striking the stone hammer with the crack hammer.

4. Work all along the lower edge, gradually working off small sections of stone.

5. Go back to the beginning and repeat, working all along the length of the edge, clearing away unwanted stone from the bottom up. Eventually you will have chipped off most of the surplus edge.

6. You can clean up the rough new edge by changing the angle of the stone hammer to make a flat chip, or by using the cutting face of the smaller 1½-pound stone hammer to dress up the rough edge.

Removing Bumps and Wobbles

Often stones that almost fit won't work because of lumps, knobs and wobbles. It's easier to strike these off and smooth out the face of the stone than to build around them, and more efficient than to discard the stone altogether. You may be able to chip these off just by setting the beveled edge of the stone hammer or the cold chisel against the base of the lump and striking home with the crack hammer. But if the stone is hard and uncooperative, use your cold chisel or point and crack hammer to chip a thin score line all around the lump, *then* use the stone hammer to break it off.

CHAPTER 12

REPAIRING A STONE WALL

A tumbled-down wall is a challenge and a school for stone workers. You can learn a tremendous amount about stones and how to put them together by repairing walls; it's good practice for more complicated projects. Moreover, repairing stone walls is, in a small way, restoring the architecture of the past. Such a project makes a good weekend restoration project for a local historical society or old-cemetery association.

Caution! Wear gloves and proceed carefully in regions where copperheads and rattlesnakes are found. Stone walls, sawdust piles and compost heaps should all be approached with care, for these vipers favor the warmth of such environments.

Common Problems

Before you begin, look the wall over for poison ivy. If you are setting to work in the early spring or late fall, the distinctive leaves will not be there to identify this plant, which grows as an erect shrub, a trailing vine or a climbing vine. All parts of the poison ivy plant contain an oil which causes inflammation, blisters and swelling when the skin comes in contact with it. Even the smoke from burning poison ivy can be dangerous. Consult your local extension agent about ways to rid your walls of the ivy before you touch a stone. Unfortunately, old walls are very often festooned with this unpleasant plant.

If your wall is free from noxious plants, study it well before you start work to discover why sections collapsed. You may have to solve more problems than just fitting stones back together, and do some remedial work to prevent history from repeating itself. Here are some common problems of old stone walls.

Animal Dens Woodchucks, foxes, squirrels and other animals find stone walls attractive superstructures for dens and burrows. Inevitably their underground mansions cave in, dragging down a section of wall. If part of your wall has fallen through den collapse, you will have to excavate the stones, fill in the tunnel and build the wall up from the base. It is sometimes very difficult to recover a large stone from deep within a collapsed burrow. Two people alternately prying up on the stone from opposite sides with 2 x 8s can lever it high enough to allow smaller rocks to be dropped in under it; the stone can then gradually be pulled or pried out on planks inserted into the hole. Rollers, crowbars, logging chains, planks, horse power—all may be needed if the stone is huge. You may choose to leave a monster stone *in situ*, if it's not sticking up into your wall space like an obelisk. In that case, fill in around and under

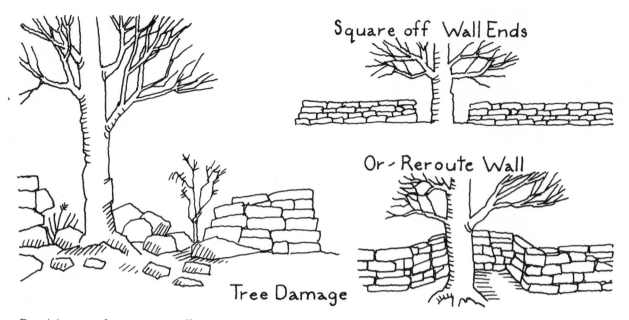

Repairing tree damage to a wall.

it with small stones and soil as best you can, and lay new base stones on top of it as though it did not exist.

Growing Tree A neglected wall will suffer over the decades from tiny treelets that sprout within its shadow, grow to sapling size and keep right on growing, their roots stretching under the wall, their trunks remorselessly thrusting apart the carefully fitted stones until the wall is breached and the stones tumble and fall into the leaves. By the time you come to repair the wall the destruction of a section may be complete, and a full-grown tree stand squarely in the line of the wall, surrounded by tumbled rocks. To cut the tree down, pull the stump and rebuild the wall is somewhat extreme. The alternatives are to construct good terminal ends on the wall on each side of the tree and leave the tree in position, or to reroute the wall around the tree.

As you start in on repairing an old wall, take care to cut back all brush and pull up other young trees that might toss your wall in the future.

Falling Branches Storms send down broken limbs and fallen trees onto stone walls that dislodge the top stones and allow rain to trickle down inside, where it freezes into ice. The expanding ice accumulates and sets more stones atilt; gradually they too find their way to the ground. You can't do anything about the fallen trees and branches of the past, but after your stone wall is repaired, make periodic inspections, especially after storms and high winds; remove any fallen branches and replace the stones they may have thrown down.

Frost Action If your wall was built badly in the beginning—laid carelessly on the ground without good foundation or drainage, or built with excessive "run"—it may have broken up in the pitching and heaving of repeated frost and thaw. Rather than rebuild carelessly, consider using the stone in a new wall built properly from a foundation trench upward. However, frost heave in cold climates will have some inevitable effects—perhaps severe—even on a well-built wall. Once the wall is rebuilt, an annual spring tour after the frost is out of the ground will reveal frost heave damage and allow you to repair it before the deterioration goes too far.

Washouts Snow-melt run-off, flooding after heavy rain, eroded gullies and hillsides, changes in water courses, all can cause washout of the underpinnings of a wall and result in its rapid collapse. If you see evidence that sections of your wall have gone down to flooding, you must improve the drainage at the trouble points. Parallel ditching the wall uphill, that is, digging a drainage ditch running parallel to the run of

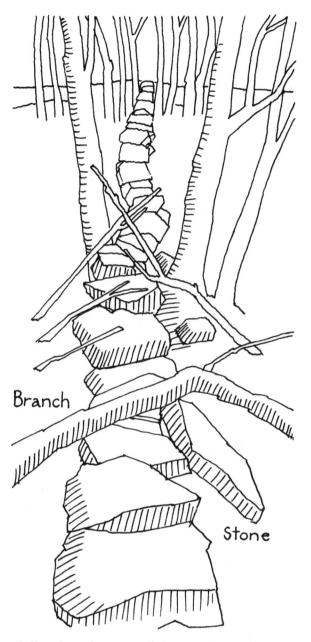

Branch

Stone

Falling branches can pull down a stone wall over the years. Part of having stone walls is a yearly maintenance check and a few days of springtime repairs.

the wall, can channel the water to a better place for its dispersal. But ditching is hellishly hard work, and ditches need a good deal of maintenance if they're not to fill up with leaves, silt, twigs and invading grass. If the water problem is confined to a relatively short section, you may want to install a tile or culvert through the wall to carry off the water harmlessly.

Rebuilding the Wall

The stones that made up your wall will be scattered along its length, often buried in the soil or moored beneath the roots of bushes and new-growth trees. As you collect and dig out the stones that have fallen away from the wall on both sides of its entire length, grub out the bushes and trees too close to the wall. While picking up your stones, glance often at the wall; the original builder's pattern of work, placement of stones, may reveal itself. By the time you finish stockpiling your working stones, you will have developed a faint sense of how they will go into the wall.

Because you are repairing an already partially built wall, you will probably not have to rework the foundation unless the damage has been extensive. But as you build up the wall, there are several important elements you should try to master.

"One-on-Two, Two-on-One" It doesn't hurt to mutter this to yourself every time you place a stone until it becomes as natural as breathing to bridge two stones in a lower course with one above, or to lay the joint of two stones on the solid foundation of a sturdy single stone. Never should a joint in one course fall directly over a joint in a lower course—gravity will finish what frost heaving begins.

If the builder has not obeyed the rule of one-on-two, two-on-one, the result is columns poorly tied into each other; each is a separate, weak unit standing precariously on its own base. The run-on joint is called "the run." Too much run is not good. Staggered, steplike runs are strong and thus desirable.

Tie Stones Walls are three-dimensional, of course, and as you build you should consider all of the forces and stresses moving against and with your wall. Building one-on-two, two-on-one literally knits stability into the length of the wall, which becomes a long chain of stony links that is both flexible and strong. But care must be taken to knit the wall together in another direction, through its breadth.

Even though it follows the rule of one-on-two, a wall whose breadth is only several stones wide doesn't have the flexibility and strength that a long interconnected chain of stones does. By setting in tie stones that go from one side of the wall to the other every few yards, the wall gains tremendously in its ability to resist frost heaves, flooding and blows from above. Tie

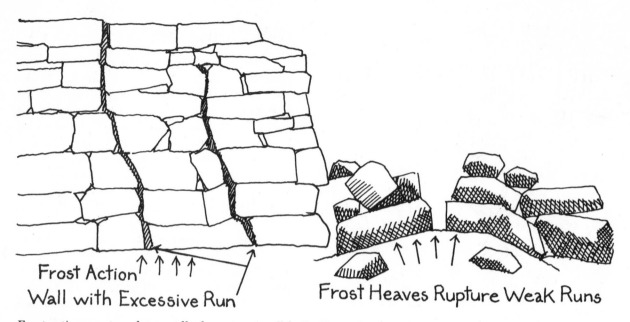

Frost Action ↑↑↑↑
Wall with Excessive Run

Frost Heaves Rupture Weak Runs

Frost action can toss down walls that are not well built. Vertical runs that cut across courses mean trouble.

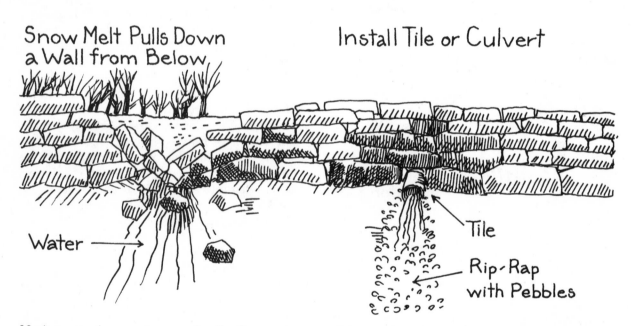

Snow Melt Pulls Down
a Wall from Below

Install Tile or Culvert

Water

Tile

Rip-Rap
with Pebbles

Moving water is a great enemy of walls. Here, spring run-off from melting snow rushes beneath a wall and undermines it. The best built wall that ever stood cannot resist flowing water that cuts under it. A tile or culvert will direct the water to avoid damage.

stones are also called *bind stones,* and bind or tie the wall together is exactly what they do. Bind stones should be worked in every 1 or 2 yards.

Batter It is bad news when rain trickles down inside a stone wall, for it collects and pools, then freezes and expands, thrusting stones up and away, finally forcing them out of true and out of line. At this point gravity becomes an enemy and pulls crooked and skewed stones down to earth again. Batter (and a roof of big cap stones) is the stone mason's effort to keep rain out of a wall. Batter means giving the wall a tapered shape, wider at the bottom, so that rain will shed off instead of dribbling inside. As a rule of thumb, batter is about a 1-inch decrease in width for every foot of height. That is, a 4-foot-high wall would be 4 inches narrower at the top than at the base. The rounder and more unstable the stones you work with,

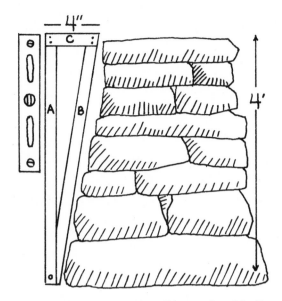

End view of finished wall, well capped and built with good batter.

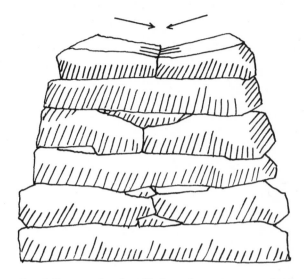

Inverted Spine

Partially completed wall shows how stones are laid to form an inverted spine.

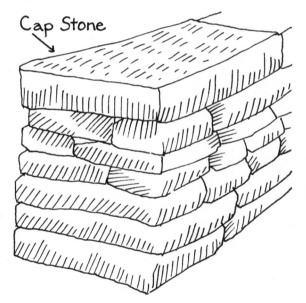

Cap Stone

The biggest and finest stones should be reserved for the top of the wall.

the greater should be the batter. Check the batter often as you build with a batter gauge.

Inverted Spine The stones in your wall should not be laid dead level, though when we look at a sturdy wall our eyes deceive us into believing it is made up of level courses. Instead, to allow gravity to help hold the wall together for centuries, build in a very slight incline from both faces toward the interior center, making a shallow V-depression along the spine of the wall. Gravity's pull then locks the two exterior faces into each other like interwoven fingers.

Cap Stones A good wall, well bound, sturdily knitted, properly battered and with indented spine, needs a roof, and this is provided with the cap stones. Cap stones should be the best and longest from your pile—the longer the stones, the fewer the joints. Take care when setting cap stones that no joint fall over a joint in the course below, or rain will seep into the vulnerable wall at this point. Cap stones have another function. Their weight and size press the entire wall beneath them downward, firming it and tying it so well to the earth that it becomes an enduring part of the landscape. Old stone workers comment that the finishing cap stones are what distinguish the expert stone mason from the amateur, for too often beginners are satisfied with small, thin cap stones that are easily dislodged.

The Fatal Flaw Besides a preference for undersized cap stones, there is another distinguishing characteristic that identifies neophyte wall builders, and that is the unfortunate tendency to be impatient. Anxious to see the wall rise, beginners will set in stones that are not right rather than spend long hours searching out the ideal stone in the rock pile, or shaping one by patient slow chipping. Or, these impatient ones will omit the foundation trench and lay their stones directly on the ground. There is no substitute for judiciousness in wall building; the work is slow, but the result will stand for centuries.

CHAPTER 13

THE GARDEN DRY WALL

Whether you use dressed stone, scrap stone from the quarries or fieldstone saved from an old wall or laboriously dug, dragged and gathered into your stone pile, one of the most rewarding projects you can undertake is to build a wall on the north side of your garden. Even a modest wall 3 feet high will make beneficial changes in the microclimate of your garden, and will improve it tremendously as an environment for growing plants, especially when the other three sides are fenced in.

A north wall of stone functions like a trombe wall in a solar house—it absorbs the heat of the sun during the day and gently radiates it back at night. This means that a garden with a stone back wall has a warmer, more equable climate, and a longer season. The warmth of the sun in early spring is stored in the wall and radiated after the sun sets, as is the fading warmth of autumn days, so growth continues here after nearby open land is cold and useless to plants. Plastic-covered frames or old windows leaned against the wall in spring and autumn make an improvised greenhouse and can add weeks to your growing season.

There are other advantages. A stone wall on the north side of a sloping garden can deflect late and early frosts, as well as chilling air flowing down the slope from above. The wall also breaks and lifts the cold north wind that can chill plants and retard growth and fruit maturation even in mid-summer. The sheltered, warmer environment provided by a north wall makes it possible for the gardener to raise more tender plants with success or those which demand a longer growing season than occurs naturally in the area.

A higher wall makes a traditional support for espaliered fruit trees or roses; old woodcuts of medieval gardens show pears, apples and cherries growing against such walls. The back wall is commonplace in European gardens, not only for privacy, but for the benefit of climate it provides. On the outside the wall acts as a barrier to domestic and wild animals, and even humans who admire the melons and eggplants with larceny in their hearts. (Although deer and goats can leap over anything under 10 feet tall, cows, horses, dogs, chickens and rabbits are deterred from invading.)

There is privacy in a walled garden. The silence and peace in the warmth, the drowsy bumbling of bees which seem to enjoy the sheltered stillness as much as the plants, the protection from the prying eyes of passersby, all increase the pleasure and value of the garden many times over.

Building the Wall

Building a stone wall is a major project that can take you an entire summer or even several summers, so approach the task in a contempla-

tive and patient mood. Draw on the techniques you've learned in mending walls, and work slowly, carefully; you are building for future generations of gardeners. Have your stone pile gathered, your tools at hand, and a few barrels of coarse crushed gravel or pebbles handy.

The Trench Lay out the precise line of the wall using stakes and stout cord to ensure that it will be straight. Try to site it where the drainage is good. Dig the trench down to the subsoil. Theoretically, in regions of deep frost, the trench should be dug as deep as the frostline, but in the northern United States that could mean as much as 4 feet of wall would lie underground! Most New England walls have only shallow foundations yet stand sturdily because a carefully built dry wall is flexible, rising and falling with frost and thaw. Don't worry if the trench is only 6 or 8 inches deep—what counts is the way you construct the wall. As you dig the trench, make sure to throw the dirt up on both sides of the excavation. Take care to make the bottom of the trench smooth and flat to seat the stones well.

The Foundation Stones Set the largest, sturdiest, flattest stones into the trench for the foundation, *after* you've put aside the best of the big flat stones for the cap stones. Lay a bind stone that spans the width of the wall from face to face at each end. Set the foundation stones about an inch apart, and do not allow them to touch. Fill in between the stones with the coarse gravel for drainage. Lay the first course of stones atop the foundation stones so that each gravel-filled joint is roofed by a stone above. This protects the foundation from any water that manages to trickle down through the interior of the wall.

Build Up the Wall Work with utmost care, laying stones one-on-two, two-on-one, slowly decreasing the wall's width for good batter, maintaining the slight inward V-form, and chinking "in" or "out," according to your preference, with small stones. Try to chink every gap and space well, not only to knit the wall snugly so as to give it solidity and mass, but also to discourage small animals looking for a home. Lay in bind stones every yard or so. It's practical to use the larger stones near the bottom courses for a more pleasing appearance as well as to save the trouble of moving them up into the higher courses.

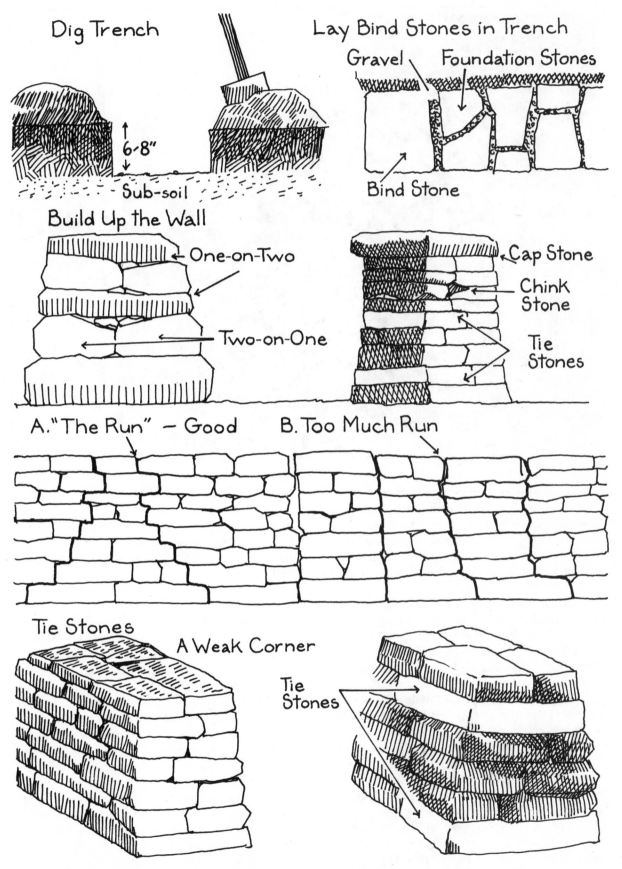

Dig Trench

6-8"

Sub-soil

Lay Bind Stones in Trench

Gravel   Foundation Stones

Bind Stone

Build Up the Wall

One-on-Two

Two-on-One

Cap Stone

Chink Stone

Tie Stones

A. "The Run" — Good

B. Too Much Run

Tie Stones

A Weak Corner

Tie Stones

Building a stone dry wall. Notice the way bind stones are used to tie the wall securely in place.

Keep the work area clear of tools and stones. To maintain a level wall with true and square lines, check the faces, ends and top frequently with your level. After the wall is above ground a foot or so, bank the base with the excavation soil, packed at an angle so that rain and melt water run off.

As the height of the wall rises, it will become increasingly difficult to set large stones in place. Don't risk strain and rupture by carrying or lifting these heavy monsters; use your planks for ramps and roll, pry or turn the big ones into place.

The Cap Stones When at last your wall reaches the height you wish it to be, put on the cap stones you have set aside. Place these large, flat stones so that they cover any joints in the course below. The bigger and heavier the cap stones are, the less likely they will be disturbed by anything, from frost to hunters walking on the wall.

Some modern wall builders like to spread an inch of fluffy portland cement mortar on the wall before setting the cap stones. This makes them less likely to dislodge. (See Appendices,

"Cement—The Heart of Concrete and Mortar.")

As a last touch you might want to sign your work; use the point and crack hammer to chisel out the date and your name. You can be proud that you are continuing the ancient skill of dry wall building.

The dry wall has several advantages over a mortared wall; its beauty and harmonious fit with the natural world, and its monumental aspect which shows that it was constructed with skill and patience cannot fail to strike any observer's eye. A dry wall is the summit of the home mason's projects. It's a pity that so many "home improvement" books skimp on advice or present erroneous information on dry walling as too difficult or too slow for most homeowners; they urge, instead, perfectly hideous constructions of concrete block, or expensive and slick-looking ashlar stone. Nor is the mess of stone and mortar poured into forms anything to write home about—it offers rapidity at the cost of quality. *By all means try your hand at dry wall building.* Recent retirees who miss the routine of work often take to stone wall building like ducks to a river.

CHAPTER 14

BUILDING A MORTARED WALL

Portland cement mortar is a wonderful substance very frequently misused. It is not a glue that will stick stones together. It cannot defy gravity and frost. A badly built wall of round or slanted stones, thrust in any which way owing to the builder's hope that the mortar will hold it together, is still a bad wall, and won't stand the test of time. Many walls built today are little more than tremendous amounts of mortar with stones stuck into it, like raisins in pudding; most of these are really concrete walls with stone eking out the expensive mix or serving as a decorative element. These are not true mortared stone walls.

The proper way to use mortar in a stone wall is as a replacement for the smaller stones and shims that fill up the interstices and crevices—mortar as a *filler*, not a *binder*. The trench and foundation work must be as painstaking as for a dry wall, the stones trimmed flat and laid carefully with the mortar sandwiched between as the yielding, plastic bed it is. The stone itself should be the basic ingredient of the wall, and the mortar simply filling.

If you live in an area of severe frost action, the mortared wall is not as structurally sound as a dry wall. The trouble with mortared walls is that they are essentially stiff, rigid structures. In the North, frost action heaves a wall, or any other structure, up and down. The dry wall, knitted together like a stony stocking, has elasticity, a resilient give, so it undulates and sinks without cracking or rupturing if it's properly built. But not so the mortared wall: upward heaves the frost and some mortar breaks; then as spring melt sets in and the frost goes out of the ground, more mortar breaks under the stress of sinking downward. In a few years crumbs and chunks of mortar are falling out of the wall onto the ground, and woe betide the builder if the stones were not well set, for they'll follow the broken mortar to the ground sooner or later. A dry wall, on the other hand, will be as good as new.

This writer spent a year taking apart a barn built a few decades ago that fell because the farmer-builder decided to skip the traditional labor-intensive dry wall and built with mortar. The frost eventually threw down the foundation—and the entire big barn. The neighbors' barns still stand on their dry wall foundations a hundred years after they were built.

In more temperate climates the mortared wall holds some advantages over the dry wall. Such a wall can be built much faster than a dry wall, skipping all the chinking and filling in of spaces with shims and little stones, for the mortar is, in effect, a thick layer of shim. Another advantage is that the niches and crannies inevitable in a dry wall which allow the entrance of driving snow and rain, and provide homes for insects, snakes and small animals, are simply not there. A mortared wall is a solid, impenetrable structure, though portland cement mortar is not waterproof. In addition, a mortared wall can be narrower than a dry wall, and does not need to be battered. It will also use about one-third less stone than a dry wall. Finally, in the right climate the mortared wall can be built considerably higher than a dry wall with safety. Most attractive to people who do not enjoy the annual ritual of mending wall, the mortared wall needs almost no upkeep in frost-free regions.

Techniques for Mortaring Stone

There are a few simple things you should know about building a mortared stone wall that can save later headaches and problems.

Mortar This is neither concrete mix nor sand mix, but ready-mix mortar, which has the dry ingredients already measured and blended; all you need do is add water. (See Appendices "Cement—The Heart of Concrete and Mortar.") Mix the mortar in an old tub or wheelbarrow, adding the water very gradually until the mortar is fluffy (fluffy for something as heavy and concretelike as mortar, that is!) and plastic. Care must be taken to get the mixture right, neither wet and sloppy, drooling down the face of the stones, nor stiff and unworkable like too-dry bread dough. It should be fairly stiff yet mushy enough to sink easily into holes and corners without being worked in with the trowel.

Mix only enough mortar for half an hour's work. Before you add even one drop of water to the dry mortar ingredients, be sure the stones you want to lay into the wall are all shaped and ready to go so that the mortar doesn't stiffen in the wheelbarrow as you chip away despairingly or search frantically for the right shape.

Gloves Do not get earthy and try to handle mortar like clay or soil with your bare hands; mortar will irritate and dry out your skin so severely that it will crack and split. Wear gloves and use tools—you'll last longer.

Stones For the mortared wall the stones must be clean and dry—soil and dust prevent a good bond from forming between stone and mortar. The stones can be hosed off and left to dry thoroughly before they are used.

Large Stones If you are setting in very large flat stones, you may need to insert a few wooden shims around the outside edges *before*

you lay the stone in to keep it from squeezing out all the mortar. The wooden shims can be pulled out after the mortar has set, and a little patch work with a pointed trowel and a bit of fresh mortar will fill the holes.

Setting Action of Mortar Don't fuss and fiddle with the mortar, smoothing it out with the trowel or pointing it up in the joints and runs—slap it on smoothly, about an inch thick, set the stones and leave it alone. Mortar doesn't dry, it *sets* in a chemical reaction, and you weaken the internal bond if you go over it. Of course, if mortar is squeezing out between the stones and dribbling down the face of your wall, you will scrape the excess off and wipe away the white stain with a big sponge and bucket of water. Catch such drips before they set— after that the stain is very hard to remove.

Once you set a stone in position in its bed of mortar, don't pick it up again and start shifting it about; the bond is stronger if the stones are left in place. The chemical reaction commences almost as soon as you lay the stone into the yielding bed of mortar.

Building the Wall

It is attention to construction, not mortar, that will give your wall its strength. If you follow the basic principles for building a dry wall, your mortared wall will stand long and strong. You need not give fanatic attention to batter or the inverted spine if you live in a frost-free region.

1. Prepare the trench and foundation stones as for a dry wall. (See chapter 13, "The Garden Dry Wall.") Pour in a bed of mortar about 1 inch thick for the foundation stones. Set the bind stones at the ends first, then the others. Fill in the joints between the stones with mortar after the stones are set in place. You need not bother to pack the interstices with gravel as in a dry wall.

2. Work in approximate courses in building up the wall, laying first an inch of mortar, then setting a stone. Follow the principle of one-on-two, two-on-one. *Be sure to dry-fit your stones before spreading the mortar in place.* Use wooden wedges under very heavy flat stones to avoid squeezing the mortar out.

3. Spread a final bed of mortar 1 inch deep and set the cap stones. Fill in the open joints after the stones are in place.

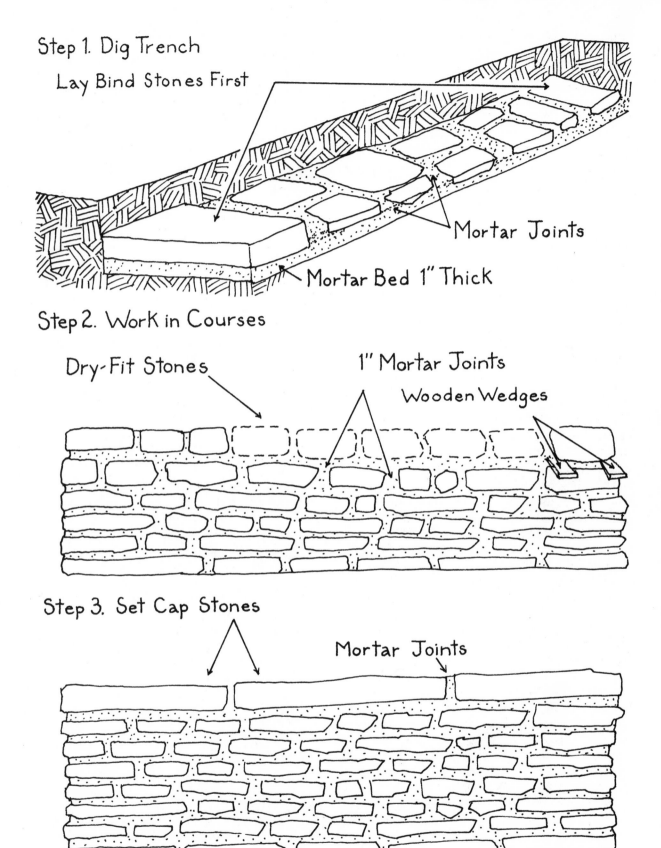

Step 1. Dig Trench

Lay Bind Stones First

Mortar Joints

Mortar Bed 1" Thick

Step 2. Work in Courses

Dry-Fit Stones

1" Mortar Joints

Wooden Wedges

Step 3. Set Cap Stones

Mortar Joints

Mortar fills the chinks in a mortared wall that would be stuffed with small scraps and chips in a dry wall.

BUILDING A RETAINING WALL

Retaining walls have a double function for gardeners. Not only do they prevent erosion on sloping ground, but they can make a series of terraced garden beds out of unused land. Dry walls are preferable to mortared retaining walls because they allow water to filter through, water that would back up behind a solid, mortared wall unless channeled away or through it with considerable extra effort, time and expense. The pressure that surface and underground water running down a slope exerts against anything blocking its way is awe-inspiring. Most people have seen 6-foot-high retaining walls built of concrete block and mortar which, despite their size and strong materials, have ruptured or bulged in the center because of the pressure behind them.

Retaining walls of any height should lean back into the slope at a good angle—they need plenty of batter. Sometimes the home improvement books suggest making a rock garden retaining wall of a single course of stones set into a slope. This may hold the soil in place, but unless you choose the stones and place them very carefully, you will have a foolish-looking, highly artificial assemblage of stones. Karl H. Grieshaber, the Brooklyn Botanic Garden's rock garden expert, writes, "A rock garden is not a meaningless jumble of rocks showing drill marks or glaring and newly exposed surface."

The Rock Garden

Some of the most striking gardens in existence are rock gardens, and the dry-built retaining wall leaning back into a slope, its crevices packed with rich soil and planted to choice specimens—whether moss pinks, candytuft and basket of gold in a sunny spot, or a fine selection of miniature ferns and mosses in a shady location—can be an imaginative and striking treatment of a problem grade. If you wish to try the dry wall rock garden which also works as a retaining wall, work in a batter of 2 inches for every foot of height, and arrange the courses so that water is channeled *into* the cracks between the rocks, thus giving the plants the moisture they need. As you build up such a wall, pack in compost and soil in the face of the structure. The plant roots will absorb water that trickles inside, preventing the buildup of expanding winter ice and excessive frost and ice heaving.

Before you begin a rock garden retaining wall, take the time to study the exposure, the site and the type of rock you have to work with. The alpine plants used in rock gardens tend to press their root systems directly against the rock. The best kinds of rock are sandstone and limestones for their agreeable pH. Granite is too acid to suit many of these plants. Avoid *113*

Single Course of Stones Set into a Slope

A very simple retaining wall of large stones set so they lean uphill. This technique has limited use, for weeds will grow between the rocks. Terraced retaining walls offer gardeners more usable soil.

windy sites and heavy shade. Rock gardens require a great deal of care and attention, as most gardeners know, so be sure you're building the best kind of environment possible for your plants.

The Brooklyn Botanic Garden's *Handbook on Rock Gardening* is invaluable in the planning stages, as is membership in the American Rock Garden Society. For ordering information on the BBG's famed series of gardening handbooks, write:

Handbooks
Brooklyn Botanic Garden
1000 Washington Avenue
Brooklyn, NY 11225

Walls and Terraces

A different retaining wall solution for a slope is a series of low retaining walls backed by level terraces which may be planted to grass or made into luxuriant flower or vegetable beds. A more beautiful setting for an herb garden, perennial border or terraced vegetable garden is rare. One can sit on the cap stones of each wall and weed or set plants in the bed just behind it. Drainage in such terraced beds is excellent. If the slope is south facing, these partially raised beds will enjoy warmer soil than even the "trombe"-walled garden. For centuries farmers in less mechanized cultures or in very

rugged land have built terraced gardens on slopes, gaining valuable agricultural land and holding back erosion on unstable grades. A few low retaining walls can perform the same function in miniature on your backyard slope, giving you productive and stable growing space.

Two or three low retaining walls backed by garden beds are easier to build, more useful and less problem-fraught than one big 6-foot wall which demands backfill, careful batter, drainage tiles and, if you live in a suburban community, a number of forms, plans, specifications and inspections before you get a permit. Even if these requirements are met you might find yourself balked by regulations from doing the job yourself, forced instead to hire a professional engineer and expensive contractors and to use poured concrete instead of stone. Better to pretend you are a peasant working your hillside plots, and build several low walls instead.

Drainage

If you decide you'd like to have a mortared retaining wall, recognize that the water that accumulates from rain or run-off behind the wall must go somewhere, either along the length of the wall to emerge at the end and be channeled into a safe outlet, or through the wall. Unless proper provisions are made to get rid of the water, it will wash out the wall or breach it. Drainage is a major consideration in a retaining wall.

Both dry walls and mortared walls that retain a slope must be backfilled with gravel or crushed stone. This lets seeping water flow along the wall and sink underneath it without washing away supportive soil behind it. Such gravel-backfilled walls have to have some sort of conduit at the ends to carry away the emerging water safely. Mortared walls must have "weep holes" installed in their bases as they're being built. Weep holes are sections of 2-inch pvc pipe set in like bind stones from front face to backfill every 3 to 6 feet. The weep holes allow water to drain away without weakening or washing out the wall. Dry walls, of course, are pierced through and through by natural weep holes.

Building the Wall

Decide whether you want a rock garden dry retaining wall, or several low walls fronting

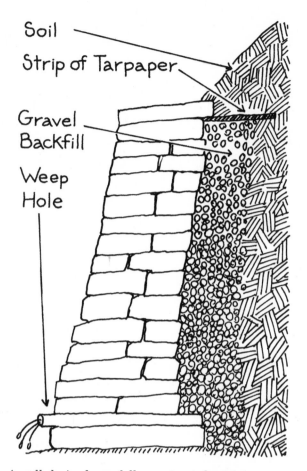

Soil

Strip of Tarpaper

Gravel
Backfill

Weep
Hole

*A well-drained, carefully constructed retaining
wall. The scale of this wall can be greatly reduced,
but the principles remain the same: batter the wall
toward the slope and provide good drainage with
gravel backfill and weep holes.*

garden beds. Study the slope you want to convert very carefully. If the slope is formidable and it looks as though there is clay soil under the sod (clay swells when wet and exerts tremendous pressure on any wall built to hold it), and you live in a suburban environment, check with your town officers for possible restrictions on your plans.

Measure the slope and the grade, and plot them on graph paper. Mark out the terraces and beds, or the rock garden wall.

1. Low terraced beds mean shifting soil from one place to another, then holding it there. Start with the lowest wall and excavate a trench as for a dry wall (see chapter 13 "The Garden Dry Wall"), but of double width to accommodate the gravel backfill. Set the topsoil aside. If the terraces are to be garden beds, incorporate the soil from the trench into several good compost heaps which can be working while you are building the walls. When the time comes to shovel all the soil into the beds, it will be of superior composition, rich and loamy and full of organic material.

2. Lay the foundation stones as for the dry wall described in chapter 13. Before laying up the wall, build a batter gauge with a backward slope into the hillside of 2 inches per foot of height. Build up the wall as you would a dry wall, but don't bother working in an inverted-V center spine. This wall is braced back against the slope of the hill. As the wall rises, fill in behind it with gravel, and behind the gravel, with soil. Stop the gravel 4 inches or so below the level of the cap stones, and run a strip of tar paper along the gravel surface to serve as a roof that will keep soil from percolating down through it and clogging the drainage.

3. Set the cap stones especially securely since they will function as the gardener's bench as he or she works in the beds.

4. Build the next walls in the same manner, working up the slope. For the sake of convenience, don't make the terrace beds more than 3 feet deep; it would be difficult for anyone but a gardener with extraordinarily long arms to reach to the back of the bed. You may, if there is room, run a narrow flagstone walk at the back of the beds and at the base of each wall.

CHAPTER 16

BUILDING STONE STEPS

Stone steps on slopes, up from a garden or onto a terrace, can be complex structures of skillful dry wall work or very simple stepping stones set securely into the earth. Four basic types useful to the backyard gardener are: steps of dry wall construction, large overlapped stones, stepping stones, and railroad ties with stones.

Consider the formality of the site before you start feverishly laying stones. A woodland walk through a wildflower garden, for example, should look as natural as possible. Here stepping stones set to fit into the natural lie of the land might be best. A formal sunken herb garden would be appropriately set off by dry wall steps. Whatever you decide to do, do it on paper first, after taking measurements of slope and grade so that you can judge how many steps of what dimensions are called for.

Use stone with a surface rough enough to be non-skid, but smooth enough not to trip up pedestrians. You may find a bargain load of polished granite slabs, rejects from the tombstone carvers because of structural flaws, but don't use them to make steps! They will be dangerously slippery when dry, and lethal when wet with rain or coated with frost. Neither use rough fieldstone with lumps and protrusions ready to catch the feet of the unwary. Trim such stones with a cold chisel and crack hammer. Shale is also undesirable for steps—thin layers

break off, and someone climbing the stairs can slip or catch his toe on the loose plates. Flat, strong stones of good size are best.

If you are planning a flight of steps, for safety's sake make all of them of the same measurement—same height of riser, same breadth of tread. There are limits to the dimensions of treads and risers; riser heights can range from 4 to 7 inches. Treads may range from 16 to 20 inches. As a rule of thumb, low risers generally go with wide treads. The average measurement for an outside stair is a 6-inch riser and a 15-inch tread. Even if you are just setting in simple stepping stones, keep these dimensions in mind.

Steps of Dry Wall Construction

Steps built like a dry wall must be put together with the greatest possible care, for not only do they suffer the pitch and heave of frost and thaw, but they must stand up to heavy traffic. Use only very flat stones that will lie evenly on those below; no oddly shaped fieldstone here.

After carefully measuring how many steps are needed to reach the top level, start with a shallow trench as you would for a dry wall. (See chapter 13, "The Garden Dry Wall.") Make the tread of the lowest step extra wide so that it *117*

Special Project
A Stone Bench

It's very pleasant and useful to have a stone bench right in the garden or under a shady tree nearby, not only as a spot for an occasional rest from weeding, but also as a surface on which to cut the first ripe melon, the rich pink-amber juice flowing sweetly, or to take an impromptu lunch of French bread, a little olive oil and sun-ripened tomatoes fresh from the vine. You'll find yourself putting seed packets, watering cans, tools and garden books on the stone bench, or offering it as a seat to a fellow gardener who's stopped by to see your delphiniums. After a few weeks you'll wonder how you ever lived without a stone bench in your garden.

Building a stone bench is probably the easiest project in this book. But you need an exceptional stone—big, thick and long—for the seat of the bench. It is worth looking for a long time to find the right stone. Good wall stones will do for the two piers at each end. Be sure to place the bench in a section of the garden where it will not be in the way of tillers or other soil preparation machinery, unless you want to take it apart and reassemble it each spring!

1. Dig trenches for the end piers. The surface of the bench should be 16 inches from ground level.
2. Build the piers up, one-on-two, two-on-one, keeping them level and true.
3. Do *not* try to lift the big stone, even with help, into place. Instead, build a double ramp of stout planks resting on each pier and braced below with rocks or log rounds, then work the stone up the incline by pry bar or rollers, and pry it into position. Be very careful; you don't want to drop this one.

Build in ¼" Downward Slope for Rain Water Run-Off

A slight downslope built into each step's position removes the dangers of standing water and thick ice.

can serve as the foundation for the overlapping riser of the next step. Try to build in a very slight forward tilt ¼ inch off the tread level, so that rain will be shed and there will be less likelihood of ice formation. Follow the one-on-two, two-on-one rule.

Large Overlapped Stones

Steps of this sort take considerable care on the part of the builder to get stones all the same size and thickness. They must be placed with precision for a smooth, even climb.

Step 1. Dig Trenches for End Piers

← Bind Stones → 6"

Step 2. Build Up Piers-One-on-Two-Two-on-One

16"

Step 3. Move Seat into Place

Rollers

Double Ramp ↘

Log

A stone bench can be as simple as a large flat stone set securely on two sturdy blocks, or as carefully constructed as the bench above, built in stone wall style.

Stepping Stones

You can get literally more mileage from your stones, if you're limited in number, by making stepping-stone stairs instead of a solid flight. These simple steps are quickly set but need more upkeep than the others. A few times in a season you will have to clip back the mat of grass roots that encroaches on the surface of the stone and will smother it in a few years if untended. If the steps are surrounded by lawn, hand-clipping around them saves your lawn mower blade from that final indignity—clanging into an unyielding stone.

Railroad Ties with Stones

Ties, paving stones and sand make a safe and attractive series of stairs especially well suited to paths and walkways. The ties are cut and set to form the riser as well as the first few inches of tread; the flat stones form the greater surface of these large "landing" type steps.

1. Level the earth surface for the first step.
2. Cut the railroad tie to fit, then drill a 1¼-inch hole at each end to take 1-inch pipe or reinforcing rod. Cut two sections of pipe 6 inches longer than the thickness of the tie.
3. Set the tie in place and hammer the pipes into the ground so that they are slightly below the surface of the tie. Fill behind the tie with a bed of sand 2 to 4 inches deep.
4. Set paving stones firmly into the sand so that they are level with the tread surface of the tie. Repeat for the next step and the next.

Helpful Sources for Stone Workers

Curtis W. Fields, *The Forgotten Art of Building a Stone Wall,* Yankee, Inc., Dublin, N.H., 1971. This book has much useful material on dry wall building, and is particularly good on quarrying and splitting stone. Some of the text is confusing, but the illustrations are worth a thousand words. Mr. Fields's terraced retaining walls are noteworthy.

Ken Kern et al., *The Owner Builder's Guide to Stone Masonry*, Charles Scribner's Sons, New York, 1980. An excellent book on stone work with projects ranging from walls to houses, written by people who have worked extensively with stone. Problems and solutions are presented with clarity and grace. The illustrations—largely black and white photographs—are murky and poor.

John Vivian, *Building Stone Walls,* 2d ed., Garden Way Publishing Co., Charlotte, Vt., 1978. Though unevenly presented, there is some useful material here. Interesting to homeowners with erosion and gully problems are the stone check dams illustrated in the final essay.

4

DRIVEWAYS:

Plan, Construct and Repair Your Own

CHAPTER 17

THE DRIVEWAY SETS THE TONE

Handsome garden patios, beautifully built stone walls, and winding brick pathways through the flowers lose their effect when visitors have to enter your property crashing and grinding their gears over a poorly situated, eroded, or potholed driveway. In the country, approaches onto the main road are often dangerously angled and obscured by thick growths of bushes and weeds. In the suburbs, drives are plagued by cracked asphalt and crumbling concrete—problems striking many homeowners as calling for the specialized and expensive services of a contractor, which they put off until getting to the front door is like driving over a terminal moraine. A well-constructed, carefully planned driveway can set off a place beautifully, but of all the types of grounds improvement and owner design, driveway planning is the most neglected.

Too many people believe that the shortest distance between two points is the only thing that counts in laying out a driveway, and they call in Joe the Bulldozer Operator and tell him, "Run it right through there straight up to the house." The terrain may be as steep as an Alp, as soft and wet as a quagmire, or in the deep boreal shade of evergreens where the snow grudgingly refuses to melt until the first blast of summer heat, but a narrow bulldozer track in a bee-line from the main road to the house is what they end up driving on.

This writer has lived at the end of some of the most fearful driveways in northern New England, and has spent many unpleasant hours chipping ice out of culverts, repairing washouts and waterbars, and trying to pry sinking cars out of the mud. She has learned the hard way that driveways can be planned and built to take advantage of the terrain, can be safe and easy to maneuver, and can be constructed in such a way that they take a minimum of upkeep and repair. Don't count on Joe the Bulldozer Operator to know how to build the best driveway for your particular circumstances without the benefit of your carefully thought-out plans and guidance.

This section covers the basics of driveway planning, construction and repairs with some attention to special rural problems, and is an expanded version of the author's article "Mending Your Way Home," which appeared in *Country Journal* in August 1979.

Although the construction of town and state highways and roads is a complicated field of engineering, the essentials of road building are basically common sense. Anyone with a feel for terrain can plan a driveway that is attractive, safe and traversable. Once the driveway is installed, knowing how to repair potholes, eliminate wet spots and correct other defects can make the difference between a few hours of annual work with a shovel and a major repair job. For example, one neighbor of mine with a steep, ungravelled dirt driveway lacking side ditches (Joe the Bulldozer Operator had built the drive *exactly* the way he was told to by the landowner) was displeased by the thick and gluey mire of mud season that not even a 4WD truck could get through. He laboriously dug several oblique trenches across the face of his drive to carry away the snow melt water. At the end of a week enormous gullies and crevasses had made his drive into a miniature model of the Grand Can-yon, and Fred the Gravel Truck Driver earned enough money filling it in to convert his front porch into a solar greenhouse.

If your property already has a bad drive-way in place, the case isn't hopeless; there's a great deal you can do to correct problems and improve the drive—you can even re-site irre-parable sections. If you have a surfaced drive-way that is deteriorating, you can probably make the repairs yourself. The trick is to understand what is causing the problems.

CHAPTER 18

PLANNING A COUNTRY DRIVEWAY

Every driveway, whether it is 20 feet long or half a mile, has a beginning, a length and an end. The beginning, or *access* of a driveway off the main road, takes careful planning to make it safe, easy to turn into or out of and to provide a good view of traffic in both directions. All states have regulations and safety standards for driveways entering onto public highways, and even the most remote hamlets will have specifications for drives that enter onto town roads. If the public road your driveway abuts is a state road, you must get an access permit from your state district highway engineer before you command the bulldozers to roll. Full details on required sight distances, driveway widths and approach arcs, as well as the specifications for culvert placement, will accompany the permit. If the main road is a town road, check with the town clerk for rules and permits. Usually an experienced person from the highway department will come out to take a look at your proposed driveway site, and he or she will turn out to be a fountain of useful information on grades, ditches, soil types and local sources for gravel. If your driveway needs a culvert (and it probably will where it meets the public road), the state or town may pay for or supply it.

Before you fix the position of the new drive irretrievably in your mind, walk the land very carefully, noting wet spots, the steepness of the grade, outcropping ledge rock, heavy evergreen timber, soil characteristics and the aspect, or direction, the land faces.

Wet spots may indicate springs or boggy areas that will demand culverts or another special drainage treatment to keep the drive passable in wet weather or in springtime. A steep grade means trouble with erosion and difficult snow removal. Moreover, icy conditions on a steep slope are likely to result in such dangerous situations as spinning tires or skidding, as well as poor control over a vehicle in emergency circumstances brought on by failed brakes, stall-outs, or meeting the garbage truck halfway up the driveway. Ledge rock can mean days of blasting and work with heavy equipment to carve a drive from the unyielding stone. In addition, a narrow driveway laid between two ledges will make a funnel for strong winds. Heavy evergreen timber or densely wooded terrain right to the edge of a drive makes a shady, pleasant road in summer, but snow can remain there stubbornly long after other drives are dry and clear. The type of soil can be important—waterlogged heavy clay drains slowly and means a wet, troublesome driveway. The aspect of a drive makes a lot of difference in the north; a drive on a north slope holds snow and ice a long time and is slow to dry out after rains. An east-

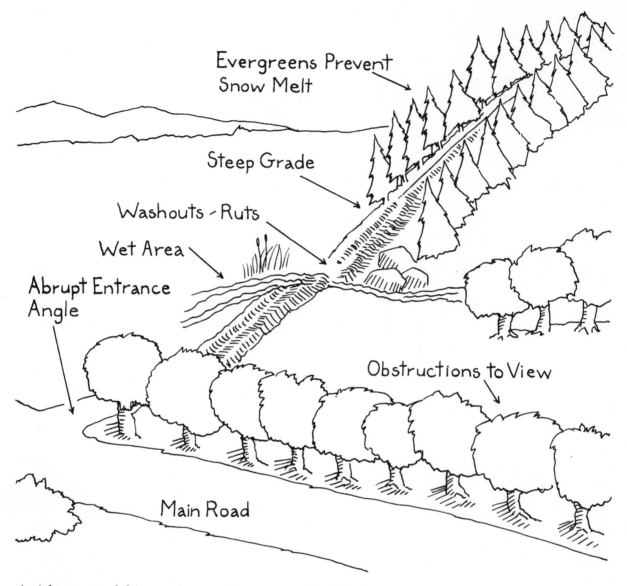

Evergreens Prevent Snow Melt

Steep Grade

Washouts - Ruts

Wet Area

Abrupt Entrance Angle

Obstructions to View

Main Road

A nightmare rural driveway, incorporating every possible difficulty.

west drive may be a groove for prevailing westerly winds.

A driveway on a south-facing slope with the tree line 75 to 125 feet away from each side, and on dry, well-drained, gravelly soil is what we all want—a drive meeting these requirements offers no trouble in construction or maintenance. Unfortunately, such ideal drives are scarcer than hens' teeth, and the longer your driveway, the more likely you'll hit a few snags that can't be avoided. But instead of blindly running a ruler line from the main road to your garage, try to pick a gently contoured, sunny open stretch for your driveway, even if it means a longer run and a curve or two, if the alternative is following steep or wet terrain. On the other hand, the shorter the drive, the less the maintenance and upkeep time involved. Aim for the happy medium.

The Access

Sight Distance The most important thing about access from your drive onto the main road is *how far you can see oncoming traffic in both directions* before you pull out onto the road. Called "sight distance," it is a crucial safety factor. Pulling out of any driveway onto a public road, even a little-travelled country road, is a dangerous procedure because of the speed differential between the car on the driveway and rapidly moving traffic, but pulling out of a driveway obscured by thick bushes or trees, steep banks or a row of mailboxes can be deadly. Many, many rural drives have poor sight distances. We've all had the hair-raising experience of driving briskly down a road when suddenly a truck or car lurches out from behind a mass of bushes, and we are forced to stand on the brakes.

Working out sight distances is quite simple, but clearing away obstructions, which can range from a giant oak to thick willow bushes, calls for hard labor. If the traffic on the public way goes past at 50 miles an hour, you must have a *minimum* view of 500 feet in both directions as your car nears the end of the drive. To measure the sight distance accurately you will need a 50- or 100-foot measuring tape and two pointed stakes that will measure 5 feet up from the ground after they are driven into the soil. (See illustration on page 128.)

1. From the center line of your driveway access measure 500 feet to the left along the public way and drive in the first stake on the margin of the road on the same side as the drive access.

2. From the center line of your driveway access measure 500 feet to the right along the road and drive in the stake *on the opposite side* of the public road.

3. Park your car in the center of your driveway with the bumper 10 feet from the edge of the public road and look down the road in each direction. You must be able to see each stake—even if it is only the top that is visible.

Unless you can see some portion of both stakes, the obstructions blocking your view have to be cleared away. If the problem is brush, a session with a sharp brush hook or power brush cutter will clear it out, but brush will have to be cut back each spring or summer as it grows anew. If the obstruction is trees and woods, the chain saw must be used. Boulders and rock ledge may require heavy moving equipment; rather than clear obstructions of this kind you may

want to relocate the drive entrance in a better place. No matter what has to be moved, don't risk a highway crash because you can't see what's coming.

The Approach Arc Most rural and suburban driveways go directly onto a public road, forcing a vehicle to swing into the far lane of the highway when entering or leaving the drive. Trucks, which have a larger turning radius than cars, will swing even farther out. On suburban streets where traffic moves slowly this is not usually a problem, but where country drives hook onto roads carrying vehicles moving at the speed limit, these ponderous and unnecessary wide turns are dangerous.

A turning arc with a minimum radius of 20 feet for cars and 33 feet for small trucks allows your vehicles a clean entry onto and departure from the public way without swinging head-on into traffic. A 20-foot radius means that the curve of the turn-in arc for a car commences 28 feet back from the edge of the public way; a 33-foot radius starts curving 45 feet back from the road edge. Plan to accommodate the largest vehicle that will use your drive. If you pilot a trailer truck for a living, or if a huge garbage truck comes up the drive every Friday, allow room for these big fellows.

The Approach Angle The safest driveways enter the main road at a 90° angle. An entrance angle of less than 50° makes turning in from the main road or out onto it difficult and dangerous. Straight, roomy, level driveways with good sight lines are the ideal.

Mailboxes While you're mapping out sight distances, angles and turning arcs, pick a safe place to set your mailbox: where it will not interfere with your view of traffic, where the mailman can pull safely off the road while he or she puts the mail in the box, and where the snowplow will not strike it down with one mighty blow of its great blade.

The Width

A long, twisty, narrow driveway up a steep slope is a nightmare, especially when you are coming down and the gas truck is coming up. A long, twisty, *wide* driveway up a steep slope is at least manageable, if not ideal. At the *very minimum* a driveway should be 10 feet wide on the straight sections and 14 feet wide on curves to accommodate truck traffic.

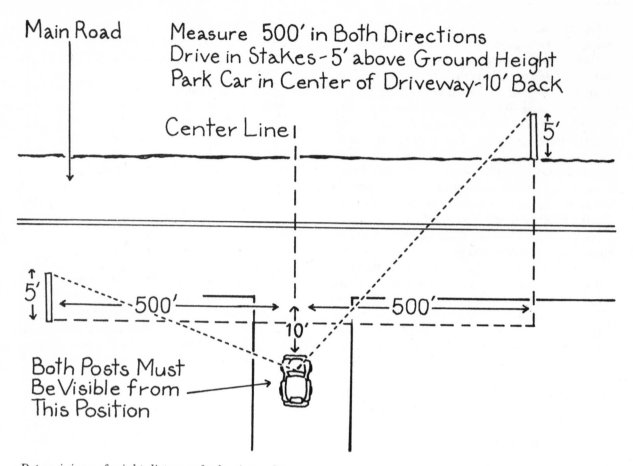

Determining safe sight distances for leaving a driveway.

Turnarounds

If your driveway is steep or long, a strategically placed turnaround is a tremendous help. In bad weather you may not be able to make it to the top of the hill. Moreover, without a turnaround the alternative is backing down the driveway, which can give you a fierce neck twinge as well as force you to back into traffic on the main road, a hazardous procedure at best. Backing down a narrow drive in snow or under icy conditions is an easy way to end up in a ditch or stuck crosswise. A turnaround gives you the choice of a dignified retreat and a safe descent, and also lets you pull off the drive when another vehicle is taking up all the room.

The end-of-the-driveway turning circle or T is, despite its convenience, a rarity in old rural drives. Rutted lawns or wide scraggly turning areas—half weedy grass and half uneven driveway—are extremely common, but give a homestead a seedy, unkempt look.

A turning circle should be marked out to allow a minimum turning radius of 28 feet for cars, or 45 feet if trucks are expected to use the drive. Make the circle drive wide and capacious. If you have a narrow drive and throw a party, your guests will have to leave in the same order they arrived, all nicely locked into place in the circle. A comfortable gravelled T outlined with railroad tie bumpers looks decent and allows easy turnaround. If you receive a lot of visitors or have a home business, a small gravelled parking lot that can accommodate four or five cars can be laid out like an extra-wide T; it will save your lawn and driveway borders from tire ruts.

The Grade

Steep drives are nothing but grief. Over the years, the money you spend on mending and repairs, the frustration and rage you feel about

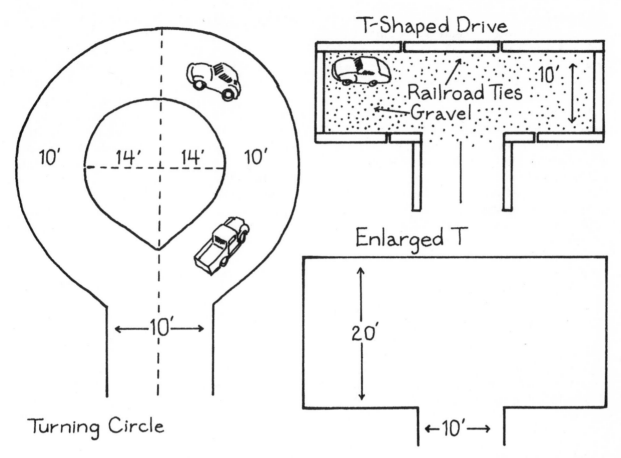

Turning Circle

T-Shaped Drive

Enlarged T

Driveway turnarounds are enormously convenient, and an hour of planning is worth a day of bulldozing.

Measuring Grade

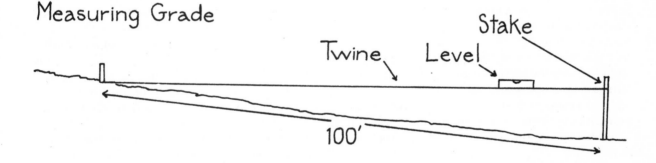

Measure Off 100' - Stake and Stretch Twine.
Make Twine Level - Measure Distance from
Ground to Twine at Bottom Stake. 1 Foot = 1%.

How to measure the grade for a proposed driveway, using readily available materials.

an impassable grade that only a helicopter can ascend in bad weather, makes a decision to have a short steep drive instead of a longer, gently graded drive a bad one. A truck with its lower gearing can get up a grade as steep as 17 percent if the surface is clear and hard, but a car has trouble with gradients sharper than 5 to 7 percent. A hard climb will take its toll of your vehicle and eat up gas voraciously. In addition, every hard rainfall will wash away gravel from the drive and undermine its base. Snowstorms that dump more than a few inches can close the drive until springtime unless you have a heavy-duty snowplow able to take the strain of operating on a steep slope. Spring snow melt will race down the drive, again carrying away your precious gravel. In short, a really steep driveway in the north can be impassable from late autumn until late spring, good for nothing but cross-country skiing. The homeowner who has to carry groceries uphill on such a driveway will bitterly rue the day the thing was constructed. On the other hand, a drive that traverses a hillside at an angle offers a gentler slope and a fighting chance at using the drive all year round.

Measuring the Grade

Squinting up a hillside and guessing at the gradient is fun, but not a good way to plan your drive. Two people, a stake, a level, mason's twine and a 100-foot measuring tape can take the guesswork out of driveway planning. (See illustration on page 129.)

1. Measure off a 100-foot length along the proposed driveway (you'll probably want to do this along the steepest part).
2. Drive in a stake at the bottom of the line. At the top of the line peg in one end of the mason's twine, then stretch it taut to the bottom stake.
3. Use the level to get the twine adjusted so that it is level.
4. At the bottom stake, measure from the ground up to the twine. A rise of 2 feet in this 100-foot length indicates a 2 percent grade. If the twine is 5 feet up the stake, the grade is 5 percent. A measurement of 20 feet up the stake (you will certainly need an extremely long stake and a tripod ladder!) represents a 20 percent

grade, suitable for mountain goats, but not vehicles.

If a few steep runs in your driveway are inescapable, make every effort to locate them at the top. By having gentler slopes at the beginning of the drive, you can get a good run going in bad weather and perhaps momentum will carry you over the crest. Be sure to place a turnaround below the steep section so that you have the option of turning around instead of backing down the entire drive.

Where the drive enters the public highway the ground should be as level as possible.

Reducing Snow Drifting

To get that desirable gentle grade, the bulldozer may have to cut your driveway deeply through the hills. A plain, straight bulldozer job will leave you with a driveway like a trench, bordered on each side with sharp, upright banks. Since nature abhors a vacuum, autumn leaves will swirl in with the wind, and windswept snow will fill up your drive with thick drifts in the first big storm. This drifting propensity can be moderated by cutting the banks back to a streamlined shape.

Driveways bordered by brush and trees are also vulnerable to heavy drifts, because the bulk of the tree trunks, branches and shrubs breaks the force of the snow-laden wind and causes it to dump its load. Tree-lined drives are beautiful, but in heavy snow country they mean you'll spend a lot of time plowing out the drifts.

You can put the same forces of nature that dump the snow to work for you. By planting windbreaks, or "shelterbelts" as they're called in the Midwest, of pine, lilac, willow or other permeable shrubs and trees 75 to 125 feet back from the center line of the driveway on the side of the prevailing wind, you force the wind to drop its snow load before it reaches your drive most of the time. However, if the storm is a bad one with exceedingly powerful gusts, or if it comes from a different direction than usual, you will, of course, get drifting.

While you wait for your living windbreaks to grow to effective size, you can accomplish the same end with strategically positioned snow fencing. The ideal windbreak—whether fence or hedge—is 50 percent permeable, just enough

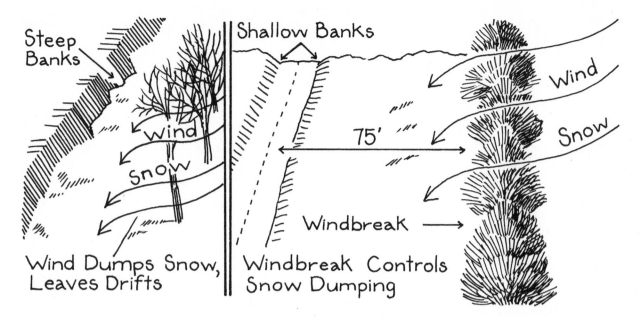

The driveway that lies like a trench between two steep banks is made for snow drifts. Careful planting of windbreak trees can control the worst drifting. It's a good idea to test the windbreak placement with portable snow fencing before planting trees. Every site will differ.

to slow the wind to the point where it drops the snow. A solid wall or fence of close-spaced boards is worse than no windbreak at all, for it causes sharp gusts and downdrafts on the lee side that can build up monster drifts. Very thick stands of pine and spruce have the effect of a solid wall; several lines of deciduous shrubs make a more effective windbreak than a forest primeval as far as driveway drifts are concerned. County extension agents have literature available on the best windbreak shrubs and trees for your area, as well as tips on how to plant them.

CHAPTER 19 _____

CONSTRUCTING A DRIVEWAY

Except for the plain dirt track gouged across the terrain by Uncle Henry on his old tractor, every driveway is made up of a base and some kind of surface material. Without a good base that lets water drain away efficiently and supports the surface material, the driveway won't last long.

The Base

The heart of a good driveway is its base, and the depth of the base material depends on the type of soil that underlies the drive.

Gravelly and Sandy Soils These types of soil have excellent natural drainage and make the best base for a drive. They have a rough, gritty feel and do not hold together well. There will probably be small stones mixed in. With this kind of underpinning, you need a base of compacted gravel only 6 to 8 inches deep to support the surface material and take light car and truck traffic with ease.

Loam Loam is a mixture of sand, silt and clay in fairly equal proportions; the stable soil that gardeners strive for, it also makes a good driveway base owing to its excellent drainage. On loam, a layer of compacted gravel 8 to 10 inches thick on top will make a stable driveway base.

Silt and Clay Silt and clay soils are sticky or greasy, fine to the touch and hold together in a ball when squeezed. Because the particles are so fine, drainage is slow and poor in these soils, and they make the worst driveway underlay. A base of compacted gravel 12 inches or more deep over this kind of soil is necessary for a stable driveway.

Gravel Most driveway bases are built up from bank-run gravel or crushed stone. Bank-run gravel contains 8 to 15 percent clay, lime, iron oxide or other fine material that acts as a binder to hold the gravel particles together. When bank-run gravel gets wet, the clay particles in the mix swell and make a water-resistant mass as well as firmly locking the coarser material in place. This swelling and tightening action keeps rain and snow melt water from dribbling down into the base and undermining the surface. The expanding and contracting mass is flexible, water-shedding and stable. If the gravel mix contains too much clay, the particle expansion during wet spells will be extreme, forcing the gravel particles out of place instead of locking them up snugly. The base will be less stable, and can easily deform the driveway into heaves and hollows.

Washed gravel should never be used for a driveway base, for it lacks the fine clay particles that strengthen and cement the mass. Washed gravel will roll, wash out and shift its position. It makes a very unstable driveway base.

The base gravel should contain no material larger than one or two inches in diameter. The

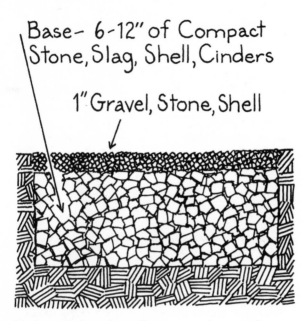

Base- 6-12" of Compact
Stone, Slag, Shell, Cinders

1" Gravel, Stone, Shell

A cross section of a well-constructed unpaved driveway.

larger the aggregate, the harder it is to bind and compact into place.

Gravel is usually bought by the cubic yard, and the price includes delivery and dumping it in place along the drive from the back of the dump truck. Check with your dealer (listed in the Yellow Pages of your telephone directory) to be sure an extra transport and spreading charge isn't added onto the quoted price. The dump truck that distributes the gravel on the drive will do a basic job, but no more. The gravel will be thick in places, thin in others, depending on the skill of the truck driver. It has to be evened out and compacted by a skilled grader or bulldozer operator after the dump truck leaves. If the drive is mercifully short and you have a strong rake and a stronger back, you can smooth and level out the base yourself, then give it a week or so to settle before adding the surface material.

Other Base Materials

Cinders In the days when everybody listened to "The Shadow" and burned "Blue Coal," the clinkers were carefully taken out of the house and dumped on the driveway. After a while they built up a good cinder base. If you are a coal burner, don't neglect this useful by-prod-

uct. Cinders are too coarse to make path or drive surfaces, but, mixed with gravel and compacted, are an excellent base material.

Slag If you live in a region of blast furnaces, take advantage of the slag by-products of the smelting process to build a driveway base. You can often get this material free by the truckload if you haul it yourself.

Crushed Rock Driveway bases can be built up of crushed rock, but bank-run gravel or other binder material must be mixed in to hold it all together.

Crushed Shell Coastal states where oysters are dredged offer their residents an unusual but very good driveway material—crushed oyster shell. Driveways built of crushed shell are snowy white and very dramatic, and many large estates are set off with oyster shell driveways curving to the portico. Unless you have a good local supply, the shell can be very, very expensive.

The Surface

There are three general types of driveway surfacing materials that can be put down over the base: natural, bituminous and concrete. What you choose depends on the climate, the terrain, the grade of the drive, the available local materials and the amount of money you are willing to spend.

Natural Surface Materials

Fine gravel, crushed stone and shell are all natural surface materials for driveways. Their flexibility makes them excellent surfaces in frost and snow climates, for they rise and fall like the dry stone wall with the frost-expanded terrain. They all offer the bite of traction to tires spinning under icy and snow-slicked conditions. The disadvantage of such loose topping is that snowplows will scrape away a certain amount of it, and spring melt will wash away more. Natural materials will have to be freshened up and replaced periodically, and thin, washed-out spots will need annual work.

Gravel This surfacing should be made up of a 1-inch layer of fine bank-run gravel over a compacted gravel base. The topping gravel should not contain any particles over 1 inch in diameter. The surfacing material will pack into the base and give a smooth, hard surface that is very agreeable to drive on after it has been ironed out by traffic.

Crushed Stone and **Shell Surfacing** Material of this type should be of fine consistency—nothing over half an inch in diameter—and may be spread directly on the compacted gravel base. Because no binding is mixed into this topping, it floats above the base. After traffic drives through, the surface material falls back into the tracks and leaves a smooth-appearing surface without the characteristic depressions of the gravel-topped drive. A floating surface will need more touching up with the rake than the gravel drive, and more of the topping will get scraped away by the snowplow and washed away by spring run-off. A floating surface is not a good idea for a steep drive, for gravity and rain will bring the material down the grade.

Bituminous Surface Materials

The bituminous surfaces are asphalt and coal tar, usually known simply as "blacktop." These are fairly expensive toppings—attractive, flexible, needing little upkeep, easy to plow in winter, and presenting a good hard surface in foul or fair weather.

If you decide to have an asphalt drive, the upper 2 or 3 inches of the gravel base should have no more than 5 percent clay in it. Having the drive bulldozed and the gravel base put in is about as far as you can go without calling a contractor. Blacktop drives should be laid by professionals who are familiar with the material, who have the specialized machinery to do the job, and whose work is guaranteed. Find reputable local contractors through the informed people in your town highway department; watch out for the travelling flim-flam artists who are here today, gone tomorrow, and offer to "blacktop" your driveway cut-rate. What you'll get is a sticky coating of aged crankcase oil, and an emptied pocketbook.

If asphalt is your preference, have the contractor look over the site and tell you what he needs in the way of a base before you start moving bulldozers and gravel around. He may prefer to add the top inches of base gravel—free of clay and contoured with a slight crown for water run-off—himself. In 1982, a driveway 10 feet wide cost roughly $100 per linear foot for a 2½-inch asphalt topping.

Concrete

Driveways of concrete are rigid, and therefore extremely likely to crack and break in a cold climate where frost heaving is common, unless special techniques are used. We've all seen those cracked and pitched concrete drives beside houses built in the 1930s and 1940s.

You can pour a short concrete driveway yourself. For a concrete driveway in the north, the gravel base should be 2 to 4 inches thick. Choose the site carefully, and be sure the drainage is superb. The less water in the ground, the fewer the frost heaves. The concrete itself should be poured 6 to 8 inches thick in a slab. Air-entrained cement is an indispensable ingredient, for the millions of tiny bubbles that riddle concrete containing this material will give it a certain amount of flexibility without sacrificing strength. The concrete becomes even more flexible, able to ride better with the surge and subsidence of frost heaves, when expansion joints are cut into the freshly leveled concrete before it has set. (Expansion joints are grooves, 1 inch deep, cut into the slab every 6 to 10 feet.) Hardware cloth embedded in the concrete gives it extra strength without making it rigid. If your climate is benign and pleasant, without winter frost, you can lay a 6-inch concrete slab drive over a 2-inch gravel base without worrying about air-entrained cement and expansion joints.

When the driveway butts onto a walk or against the house or garage foundation, it's a good idea to fill the joints between the drive and the older structure with a waterproof bituminous joint filler, available at building supply and hardware stores.

Driveway Drainage

Crowns

Driveways should not be perfectly flat strips no matter what material they're built from; they must be shaped to shed water. A center-line crown is the most common way to get water off the road surface in a hurry. Gravel drives should have a crown slope of about half an inch per foot. This means that a gravel driveway 10 feet wide will have a crown 2½ inches higher than the outside road edges. Blacktop or concrete drives, with their hard, impermeable surfaces, need a crown slope of only ⅛ inch per foot. The 10-foot-wide asphalt drive will have a center-line crown ⅝ inch higher than the outer edges of the drive; it requires a slope of only 1/16 inch per foot.

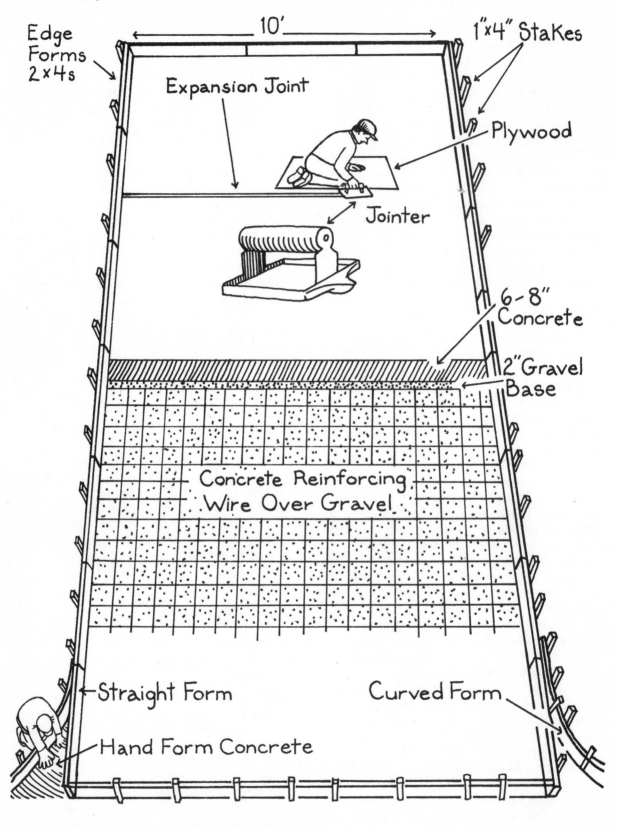

Edge Forms 2×4s

10'

1"×4" Stakes

Expansion Joint

Plywood

Jointer

6–8" Concrete

2" Gravel Base

Concrete Reinforcing Wire Over Gravel

Straight Form

Curved Form

Hand Form Concrete

Street Access

Making your own concrete driveway (if you live in a warmer climate) is a big project, but can save you a good deal of money. It is definitely not a beginner's first project.

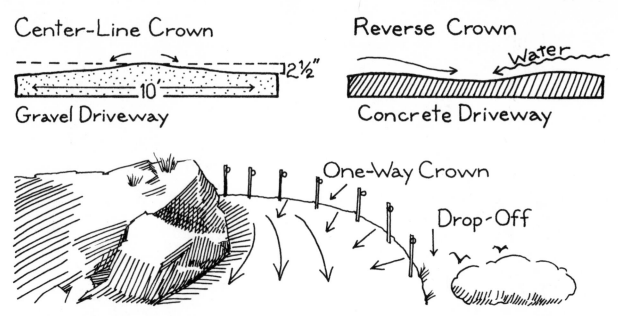

All driveways have crowns that lead surface water away. Driveways with ditches on each side have center crowns that shed the water away from the road center and into the ditches; suburban drives are often built without ditches, and these have reverse crowns that lead the water away down the center to a drain; one-way crowns, found often on roads traversing hillsides, lead the water to a shallow ditch on the downhill side to prevent erosion of the outer road margin.

There are other types of crowns for special situations. Asphalt or concrete drives laid where it is impossible to have ditches on either side of the drive—a fairly common situation in suburbia—can have a *reverse crown* down the center line which acts as a drain that pulls the water down the middle of the drive and channels it safely away. In steep, mountainous country, a road with a drop-off on one side may have a one-way crown on the edge of the drive nearest the drop-off. This prevents the road from eroding and crumbling along the outer edge, a condition that can rapidly deteriorate into washouts and a collapsed road. If you're building a driveway in hilly country keep the one-way crown in mind; it can save your life.

Ditches

The longer your driveway, the more vital are ditches. There should be a ditch at each side of the drive to carry away rain and melt water. Without ditches the water will saturate the soil at the sides of the drive and eventually flood the gravel base and the soil underneath the surface. Washouts and broken road surfaces are the price you pay for not ditching.

Ditches should be as shallow and wide as possible to reduce erosion. The worst ditches are steep and narrow—the force of rushing water can eat away the drive from underneath. There are no prescriptions and ideal measurements for driveway ditches, however, for each drive has its own special demands. Country driveways built on good soil that drains freely rarely need ditches deeper than 1 or 2 feet. On a moderate slope where the ditches fill with racing water after a heavy rain, erosion can be a headache. There are three ways to handle ditch erosion:

Rip-Rap

Rip-rap is broken quarry rock. This rock, thickly lining the sloping banks and bottom of a ditch, holds the soil in place. Rip-rap cannot be just dumped into the ditch; the stones have to be thrown into place close together. It's not precision work, but it takes time. Sometimes very beautiful rip-rap work is seen on river banks where gigantic stones have been precisely fitted together. You can, of course, make your ditches marvels of intricate stone mosaic if time hangs heavy on your hands.

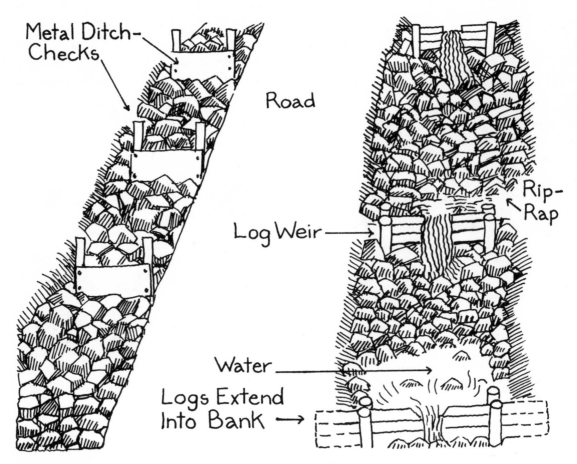

Metal Ditch-Checks

Road

Log Weir

Rip-Rap

Water

Logs Extend Into Bank →

Homemade ditch-checks of metal roofing keep spring torrents from gouging ditches into little Grand Canyons.

Ditch-Checks

Ditch-checks slow the tumultuous descent of water down long, steep ditches. These are actually miniature holding dams or weirs, with tiny reservoirs behind them when the rain comes down. The classic old ditch-checks were built of fir or cedar logs, and there were usually several of them on a bad pitch. You can improvise ditch-checks with sheets of old roofing metal cut to fit between upright posts driven into the ground. They are fast to put up and long lasting, though not so rustic and handsome as the timber weirs.

Culverts

Sometimes not even a ditch is enough to carry off excessive water flow. In wet, clay soils, in swampy areas, in places where small rivulets and streams intercept the drive, and in low-lying sections, a culvert may be needed. In the old days many culverts were hollow spruce logs, and you can still see these inexpensive drainage pipes in use on logging roads in the Northeast. More substantial were the stone culverts that were built under country roads in the last century. These were carefully laid up into four-sided tunnels from massive stones. They were strong and durable; this writer's town still has stone culverts in service that are well over a century old. Modern culverts are corrugated tubes of heavy steel, and they come in a great range of sizes and lengths.

You will almost assuredly need a culvert at the point where your driveway joins the main road. The public highway, whether state or town, will be ditched on both sides. A culvert under your driveway allows the water to continue its flow unimpeded. The town or state will usually supply and install such culverts. In some towns you pay for the culvert but the town will install it without charge. On the driveway itself, you are responsible for the cost of both the culvert and its installation.

If you need a culvert or two on the drive, putting one in is not a simple procedure that can be picked up from a book. Each situation has to be tailor-fitted with the correct size and type of culvert placed at just the right angle to carry water away efficiently. The highway department can help you with advice and specifications. These people are knowledgeable, and very helpful. Usually they will come out to your place, walk the site of the proposed driveway, and tell you exactly what you need and how to put it in.

Special Project
A Small Bridge

You have found the perfect place to build a summer escape cottage. It's fairly secluded, but not too far from home base. At any opportunity you could pick up and go there for an afternoon or a weekend without losing a half day, or even an hour, in traveling time. You drive out of town on a secondary road to a lane bordered with wheat fields; turn into it and continue for a few hundred yards and there it is— several acres of tree-shaded paradise. Unfortunately, it lies on the other side of an 8-foot-wide creek. And the water is just deep enough to drown the motor of the family car. You can't drive to the property without a bridge.

Before you give up the dream, consider building the bridge yourself. If the thought dismays you, it may help to know that people in rural areas frequently build small bridges, as they have for centuries. Banish those visions of construction crews equipped with cranes to hoist the needed materials. You and family or friends can handle the job nicely with common tools and readily available logs, planks, railroad ties and gravel.

In truth, many ideal homesites are bisected by a small waterway. In fact, the water might be a major attraction, but it is not always conveniently located.

Sometimes the driveway has to go over a brook or small stream. Steel beams and girders as supports for the driveway bridge are not necessary. The abutment and tie log construction suitable in this situation is similar to that of a railroad tie retaining wall (see Appendices, "Railroad Ties") and is designed as much to hold the stream banks in place as to support the bridge stringers and planking. (Anybody who has ever built a log cabin will find the job a piece of cake.) This bridge design is *only* for spanning small brooks not more than 6 or 8 feet wide. Bridges crossing bigger waterways involve more complex engineering techniques with trusses and reinforcement.

The logs for bridgework should be fir, cedar or other wood type that can last many decades in the damp atmosphere. All the logs must be peeled. The tie logs should be a minimum of 8 to 10 inches in diameter, and must extend deep into the stream bank—8 or 10 feet. Railroad ties and old telephone poles are ideal.

The abutment logs—peeled fir or cedar, telephone poles or railroad ties—are notched to lock into the tie logs at right angles. The layers of logs—alternating tie logs and abutment logs— are built up to the correct height, then stringer logs at least 10 inches in diameter are notched and set in place every 3 feet on center. The notches in the stringer logs should only be 2 inches deep. The stringers are fastened into place as railroad ties are held together—with metal rods or pipe driven into drilled holes.

When the stringers are in place, the planks can be laid. The planks should be preservative-treated, sound new lumber at least 2 inches thick. Often bridge planks are left unnailed for maximum flexibility, but you can nail them in. Lay them crosswise to the stringers.

Finally, 4 to 6 inches of bank-run gravel is spread and compacted over the bridge planks to make a smooth surface level with the road.

The classic stringer bridge still used by loggers and rural folk with woodlots.

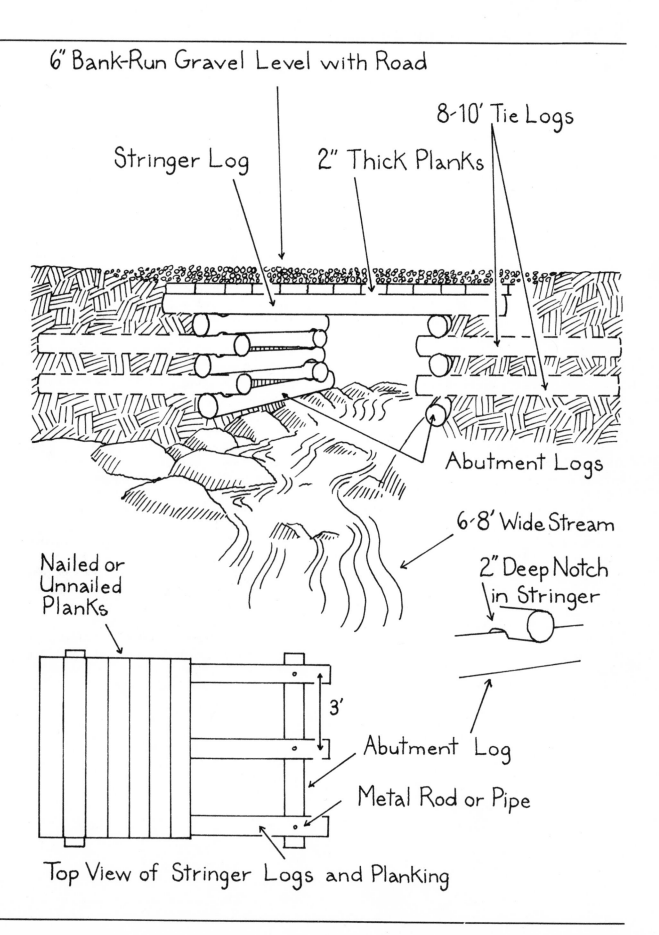

6" Bank-Run Gravel Level with Road

Stringer Log

2" Thick Planks

8-10' Tie Logs

Abutment Logs

6-8' Wide Stream

2" Deep Notch in Stringer

Nailed or Unnailed Planks

3'

Abutment Log

Metal Rod or Pipe

Top View of Stringer Logs and Planking

Special Project The Corduroy Road _____

When people hear that I once constructed a road of my own, many look at me in wonderment. They seem to be thinking of a ribbon of cement or macadam that goes on for miles. My road was nothing of the kind and it ran little more than a few hundred feet. However, it was a crucial distance over a couple of boggy acres that couldn't be bypassed. Merely leveling a lane wide enough to accommodate the occasional passage of a panel truck wouldn't do. The truck usually carried a heavy load over that stretch. Every time it did, the truck sank right down to the hubcaps, with wheels spinning helplessly in the mush.

I built a road through there because I had to do it. It was not a project of choice. However, the alternative was a dismal future dotted with stranded vehicles strongly resisting rescue. The corduroy road was the simplest answer to a problem that surely wouldn't go away by itself. There were plenty of the necessary materials free for the taking and willing neighbors to lend a hand. It took a while, and we didn't do the job all at once, but my road did get built. Only then did I realize how much having the road improved the quality of my life.

If, heaven forbid, your driveway has to go through a swamp or marshy area, or if you find yourself bogging down in wet spots as you haul your winter firewood out of the woodlot, constructing an old-fashioned corduroy road can give you a decent, traversable roadway for many years.

A corduroy road is really a floating bridge of logs that lies on a thick mattress of fine twigs and branches. The twig underbed distributes the weight of a tractor or car over the swampy area. Distribution of weight is the point of the corduroy road.

The base of the corduroy road is the thick twig underbed. This cushion should be 12 feet wide and *at least* 6 inches thick. Vast armloads of swamp brush and twigs—willow and alder will be in rich supply—are cut and laid directly on the surface of the swamp at right angles to the direction of the drive. (Twig mattresses laid in the other direction are bouncier and more unstable.) The twigs should be fine and closely packed. Large branches and tree tops are not usable unless they are trimmed down.

Long pegs of cedar driven into the mattress at frequent intervals keep the twigs from shifting about or spreading thin. The pegs are very important and shouldn't be omitted.

Small peeled spruce or fir logs, 4 to 6 inches in diameter, are then laid crosswise on top of the twig mattress. They should also be pegged in place to keep them from shifting or rolling. Choose the straightest logs you can.

At last, on top of the logs and running in the direction of the road, 2 x 6 planks are nailed on. Heavy timbers and massive planking are not good on corduroy roads, because the lighter the roadway, the better it floats. A heavy superstructure above the mattress of twigs will gradually force it down into the bog. To keep the road floating light, high and dry, no gravel is spread over the planks.

If you do make a corduroy road, always drive on it with extreme care. In rainy weather the exposed planking will be slippery, and a skid could send you into the bog.

This corduroy road construction is very ancient, except for the modern milled planks on the surface. It is still the cheapest and best way to get a driving surface through a swampy area.

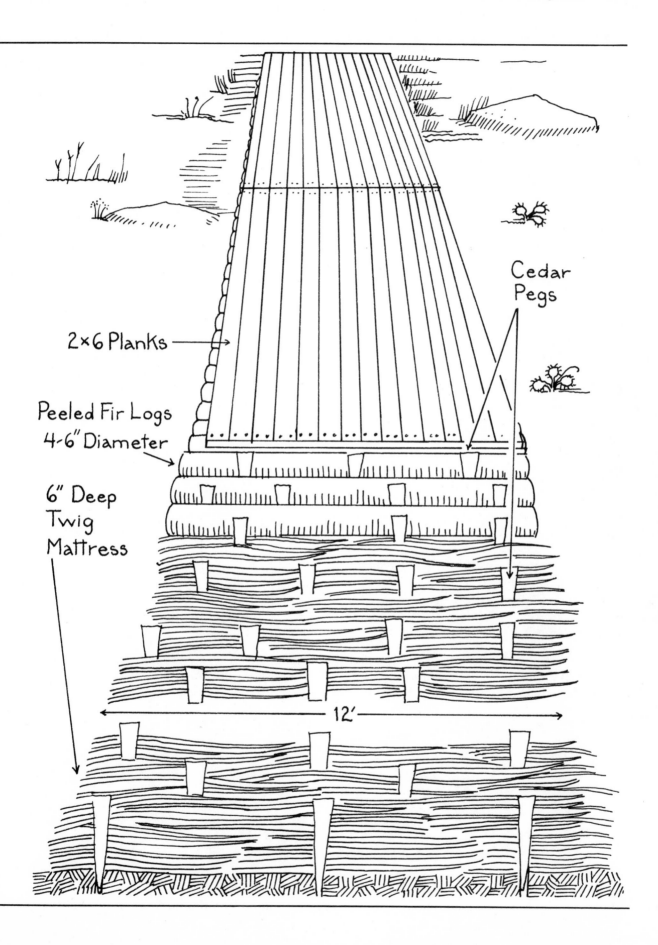

Cedar
Pegs

2×6 Planks

Peeled Fir Logs
4-6" Diameter

6" Deep
Twig
Mattress

12'

CHAPTER 20

MAINTAINING AND REPAIRING DRIVEWAYS

There may be some things in this world that will last forever, but a driveway, no matter how well made, is not one of them. Do the best you can in constructing your driveway; then, when it's all finished, start watching for the first signs of needed repair. You won't have to wait long.

Problems of Gravel Drives

Gravel drives are heirs to a thousand ills—potholes, humps, strange rocks that work their way up from the bowels of the earth to a cunning position where they are able to tear out your exhaust system. Washboard surfaces that jar your teeth to their roots and washouts after a heavy rain are not unusual. Gravel drives need upkeep and sharp surveillance. A problem corrected as soon as it's spotted can save you hours of hard work and loads of gravel.

The best time to work on a gravel drive is in the spring after the frost has gone but while the road is still damp and workable. You will have to renew the surface of a gravel drive every few years. Usually this is a case of spreading and leveling gravel in several eroded sections, not an entire resurfacing. Here are some common problems and how to handle them.

Bank Erosion

A new driveway presents raw earth to the heavens on shoulders and ditch banks, and the first deluge will carry away much topsoil and start the steady, downhill process of erosion. This action has to be checked to prevent scarred, gouged gullies and the loss of precious soil. As soon as the bulldozer turns the corner for home after shaping your new driveway, get out there and seed down the raw soil with clover, grass, vetch or other cover plants. Spread the newly seeded banks with old hay or mulch to keep the soil in place and moist while the seeds sprout and gain a foothold.

Brush

As fast as you cut it, it seems, alder, willow, wild cherry, osier, sumac and elderberry grow back, fiercer and more vigorous than ever. In just a few weeks newly sprouted brush can choke your ditches, impede your approach view and claw the finish off your car as it goes up and down the drive. In the winter this brush will act as a snow fence and break the wind so that it dumps its load of snow in the drive. So, make it an annual ritual to march on the brush sprouts with a sharp brush hook and keep it cut back.

Potholes, Ruts and Washboards

These inevitable blemishes appear on all long gravel driveways. The solution is grading or backblading with a bulldozer by an operator who knows what he's doing. Bad holes and ruts can be worked smooth by adding some bank-run gravel, preferably of the same composition

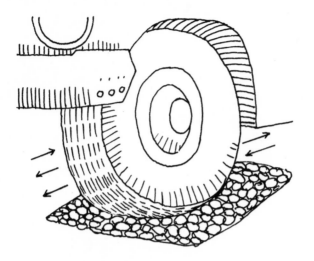

Tamping Gravel

Driving back and forth over a filled-in pothole is an excellent way to tamp down the gravel.

as the original driveway gravel for good bonding. Grader work is usually done after a rain or a damp spell when the driveway material is moist and will compact easily. If you live in the country, there are usually a few bulldozer operators around who do local dozing jobs on weekends to supplement their regular income. Some towns, if their road repair schedule is not too pressing, contract to do local work, usually at the going price in the area.

Huge Mudholes

Sometimes a spring erupts in the middle of the driveway, or flood conditions leave a gaping chasm. The worst thing you can do is to fill up this crater with rocks and stones. Such a solution is strictly temporary. Since the wet condition that caused the problem is not solved, you will find another monster hole beside the original pit in a few months.

If the problem is a simple washout, fill the hole with bank-run gravel and compact it thoroughly. You may have to add a few more inches after the first load settles. If the slope is steep and long on this portion of your drive, a *water-bar* above the washout area can divert extreme rainfall to the ditch before it has a chance to cut open the drive's surface. A waterbar is a diagonal, downhill ridge 2 inches high of com-

pacted gravel built across the drive. Waterbars make bumpy driving, but they can be effective water diversion courses where culverts won't work.

If an erupting spring is doing the damage, you can fling in mountains of gravel to no avail. A culvert is needed to carry the spring water away from the drive. The highway department of your town can advise you on the type and size of culvert required to make this repair.

Problems of Blacktop Drives

Blacktop driveways have their own peculiar problems. As they age, they become brittle — the edges crack and crumble away, the surface breaks up and leaves jarring potholes. Frost action can give asphalt drives the contours of a roller coaster, and oil, gasoline and exhaust fumes all break down the surface. On the public road the high volume of traffic literally kneads the asphalt surface with its rubber tires. This massaging action keeps bringing the asphalt binder to the surface and keeps the highway alive and flexible. Driveways, with their low volume of traffic, enjoy no such massages. Gradually their undisturbed surfaces oxidize and harden to a shiny grey appearance. If your driveway has this brittle sheen, there is not much asphalt binder on top. It needs sealer.

Brittle Sheen

A coat of tar emulsion driveway *sealer,* available at discount, hardware and building supply stores, will put a layer of binder back on your drive. The sealer will give the drive a longer life. A fresh new asphalt drive should have several coats of sealer applied after the surface has cured three or four weeks. Every three years or so fresh coats of sealer should be applied to an asphalt drive to keep the surface fresh and smooth.

Old asphalt drives can be sealed if they are not broken and badly cracked. Sweep the driveway clean with a sturdy push broom, and remove any crumbling bits of asphalt. Oil and grease drips should be scrubbed away with hot water and detergent, or any of the several oil-removing compounds sold specifically for this purpose in hardware stores. The entire drive should then be hosed down until it is quite clean.

The tar emulsion sealers are applied to the driveway surface while it is still damp. Special

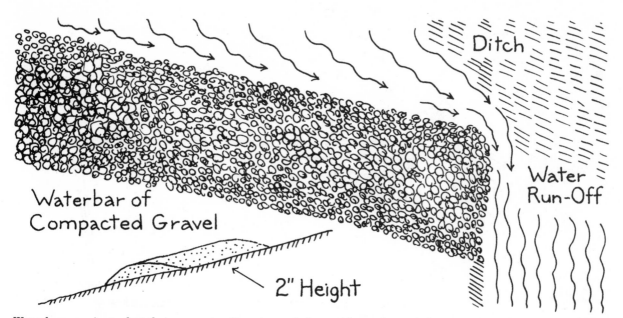

Waterbars are just what their name implies—tamped-down ridges of gravel that cross a roadway on a slight diagonal where slopes are steep, and divert rain and melt water off to a ditch on the side.

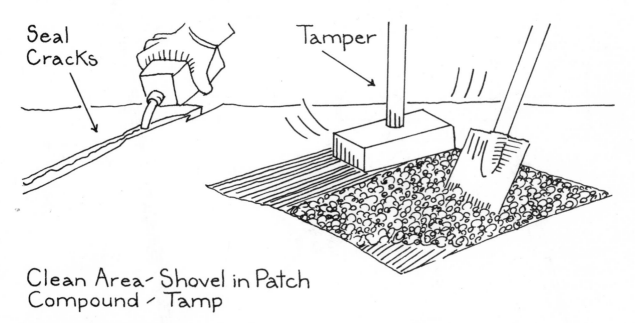

Mending a cracked and potholed asphalt driveway is a job any home repairperson can do. Hardware stores, discount stores, and building supply stores carry compounds and sealers.

brooms and squeegees for different application procedures are recommended by the manufacturer of each brand. Read and follow the directions on the label carefully; what works well with one sealer is all wrong for another. One gallon will cover about 80 square feet of driveway.

The weather is important to a good sealing job. Check the weather forecasts and choose a day that offers at least 24 hours of dry weather.

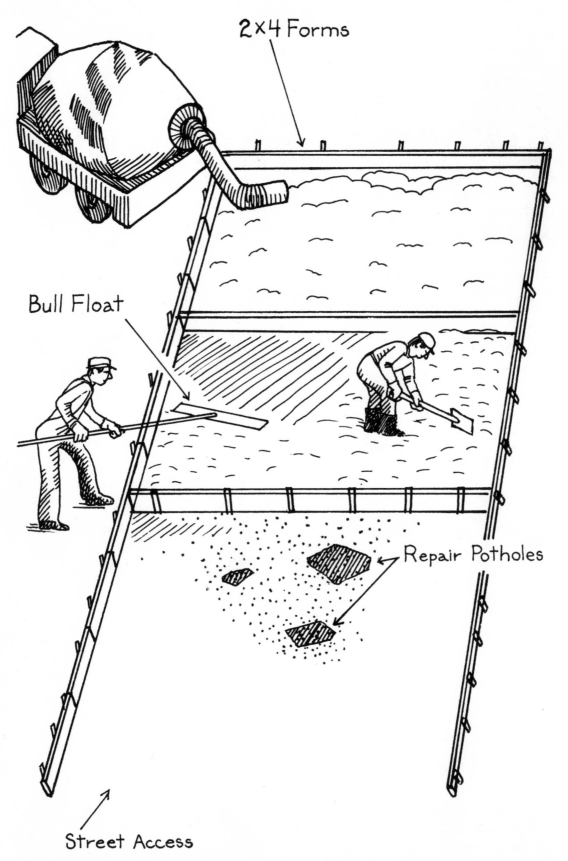

2×4 Forms

Bull Float

Repair Potholes

Street Access

The idea of tackling a new concrete slab over a badly cracked and worn drive shouldn't frighten you if you've worked with concrete on several previous projects and can build the forms.

Extremely hot or cold weather makes it hard to apply sealer correctly. The best time for repairing and sealing asphalt surfaces is a cool, dry autumn day. This timing also gets the drive in shape for the vicissitudes of winter.

Cracks and Potholes

If your asphalt driveway is cracked and pocked with potholes, you must repair the damage before you apply a sealer. Making such repairs is an easy job, as shown on page 147.

Flexible bituminous compounds for filling small cracks now come in caulking gun containers as well as cans. They are easy to use and seal up a crack before it starts to crumble into grainy fragments. Big cracks, holes and deteriorated patches from yesteryear need something sturdier. Special patching materials called aggregate, asphalt compound or asphaltic concrete come in 5-gallon cans all ready to use. The problem area is cleaned up and all loose material swept away, then the patch compound is shoveled right into the crack or hole and tamped down level and firm. This material, which we've all seen used on blacktop highways by mending crews, makes a hard, strong patch that will carry traffic as soon as it's tamped into place.

Concrete Drive Wear

If your old concrete drive is worn, cracked, broken or disintegrating on the edges, it can be resurfaced with a fresh concrete slab or with an asphalt layer. A contractor should do the work of putting asphalt topping over old concrete, but you can pour your own concrete slab directly over the old one if you feel confident mixing and working with concrete. If the job is large enough, you probably will want to call the concrete mixer truck to dump the pre-mixed material into your forms.

The old surface should be cleaned thoroughly before new concrete is poured. If you live in the north, air-entrained cement is the only thing to use. The new concrete slab should be at least 2 inches thick. There are epoxy resins available at building supply stores that form a true chemical bond between the old surface and the new concrete poured on top of it; the advantage of using the resins is that the new concrete layer need only be half an inch thick. The driveway underneath must be in fairly good shape, with all holes and big cracks repaired. There are also new epoxy-resin surfacers used to freshen up public sidewalks, parking areas and the like, but these are very tricky to use; they harden rapidly and have to be kept in tubs of ice while they're being spread.

Patching

Plenty of the mottled and piebald concrete drives around have been patched with asphalt patch mixture; these hasty repair jobs look unattractive, but they are functional. However, you can buy pre-mixed patching concrete or mix your own with cement, sand and water, and do a sturdy, good job of repairing that doesn't wound the aesthetic sensibilities. It only takes a few minutes to mix up a batch of patching concrete. If you do make annual repairs on a concrete driveway, you'll only use a bit of the cement in the bag each year, and it is important to store it someplace very, very dry, perhaps inside a plastic or metal garbage can with a tightly fitting cover. Storing an opened bag of cement in even a dry shed is disastrous, for a rainy spell will saturate the air with enough humidity to set the exposed cement.

Make driveway repairs, whether your road is gravel, concrete or asphalt, when you first notice the problems. It will save you money and time, and make going to the mailbox a safe spin instead of a pothole gauntlet.

APPENDICES

CEMENT—THE HEART OF CONCRETE AND MORTAR

An English patent granted in 1824 to Joseph Aspdin marked the formal entry of portland cement into the construction trades. Aspdin called it "portland cement" because its color was identical with a certain kind of stone found near Portland, England. The cement is made from a powdered mixture derived from limestone, cement rock, cochina and oyster shells, clay, iron ore, shale, sand and marl. Other ingredients are often added to make special types of cement for certain conditions. One beautiful type is *white porcelain cement*—a snowy white substance used for striking architectural effects. A type important to northern builders is *air-entrained portland cement*, which has the ability to form millions of tiny bubbles of air in the concrete or mortar mass, making it more flexible in freeze-thaw conditions. Air-entrained concrete and mortar are resistant to the salt and chemicals used for melting snow and ice, and they are easier to work with a trowel. If you live in the north, air-entrained cement is the only kind to use.

In the nineteenth century a type of limestone was discovered near Kingston, New York, on Rondout Creek, which made a concrete even stronger than portland cement. It was called *Rosendale cement,* and was used to build the Brooklyn Bridge and the Croton Dam, but despite its superior structural qualities its slow drying time eventually pushed it off the market.

Concrete Concrete is made out of portland cement, water and some economical fillers such as coarse sand and aggregate stone or gravel. In the projects in this book, concrete is used for footings under walls and garden structures, though its application in our civilization is ubiquitous and enormous.

Masonry Mortar Masonry mortar is used to bond bricks, stone and concrete in the projects this book describes. It is made of portland cement, water, fine sand, hydrated lime and other air-entraining substances. Masonry mortar is more plastic and flowing than plain concrete.

Mixes Mixing cement, sand, water and additives, including latex and epoxy, to make concrete or masonry mortar is like mixing vast and heavy pancake batters. There are scores of different mix recipes to suit all sorts of uses and purposes. In this day of pre-packaging and instant mixes, it's not surprising to find that both concrete and mortar come already mixed and packaged in patch-up kits as small as 5 pounds. The home mason can go to any building supply store, pick out the right package, take it home, add water, stir, and use it.

A special mix called *masonry cement* contains the correct proportions of portland cement and hydrated lime to which you add fine sand and water to get masonry mortar. This mix usu-

153

ally is air-entrained for better handling qualities.

Sakrete is a brand name, like Kleenex, for all sorts of packaged mixes such as mortar mix for laying brick and stone, sand mix for patching concrete, and epoxy and latex mending mixes.

Providing the ultimate in pre-mixed materials, *the concrete truck with the revolving drum* comes to your job and pours its load into the waiting forms. If you have extensive footings or a patio slab to be poured, this is an easy and fast way to get the job done. Homeowners with smaller projects can order as little as 1 cubic yard of concrete to be delivered. Remember that 1 cubic yard is the same as 9 cubic feet—quite a lot of concrete for a small backyard project.

Recipes

When the minerals in cement are mixed with water, they make a grey paste which sets fairly quickly and hardens into a stony mass. The hardening process is a chemical reaction between the water and the minerals, and is known to those who dabble in cement as hydration. Sand, gravel and small aggregate stones are added to extend the basic cement-water batter, an economical move that sacrifices very little strength unless, as often done by corrupt construction racketeers, a great deal of cheap sand is combined with very little expensive cement.

One cubic foot of masonry mortar will suffice to lay about 30 bricks, and this is about the maximum amount you can work with before it starts to set. Thirty-one pounds of masonry cement, 100 pounds of dry sand, and about 4 or 5 gallons of water make 1 cubic foot of masonry mortar. Since it's impractical to weigh out the materials at home, most masons working on small projects measure by the gallon, and use a strong, galvanized 2-gallon pail or a bottomless measuring box to get the correct proportions.

Mortar

This recipe is suited to all the brick and stone projects in the book.

31 pounds of masonry cement or 2½ gallons of masonry cement
100 pounds of dry sand or 7½ gallons of dry sand
water, just enough to make the mixture plastic and handle well with the trowel

Another way of measuring for this recipe is:

1 part masonry cement
2¼ to 3 parts loose, damp mortar sand
water, just enough to make the mixture plastic

If you don't want to use pre-mixed mortar cement, make your own mix from scratch.

1 part portland cement
1 part hydrated lime
4½ to 6 parts dry sand by volume

Concrete

Here both sand and aggregate stone (graded sizes ranging from 1½ inches in diameter to very tiny pebbles) are added to the cement and water to make a basic concrete mix. A 1:3:6 mixture of cement, sand and aggregate is a standard footing recipe. This is considered a lean mixture because of the relatively scanty amount of cement in proportion to the sand and aggregate.

To make 10 feet of footing 6 inches deep and 12 inches wide, you need:

⅘ bag of cement
2⅖ cubic feet of sand
4⅘ cubic feet of aggregate stone

The bottomless measuring box, which holds 1 cubic foot of material, is the most handy way to measure these amounts. You can graduate the box in fifths by marking the interior with lines every 2⅖ inches; each line represents 20 percent or ⅕ of the box's volume.

This recipe makes 5 cubic feet of concrete. (In mixing concrete and mortar, the sum of the parts is not equal to the whole—water reduces the volume of the parts.) Five cubic feet is a lot of concrete to mix by hand; you may want to rent a small cement mixer if the footings are extensive. The maximum amount of concrete you can mix by hand is 1 cubic yard, and that is hard going, for you must shift and mix 1,000 pounds of material until it is well blended.

A recipe for a somewhat richer mixture designed to bear a heavier load is the 1:3:5 mix.

1 bag of cement
3 cubic feet of sand
5 cubic feet of aggregate stone

The Bottomless Measuring Box

This simple device makes measuring cement, sand, lime and stone easy and accurate. The interior of the box should measure 12 x 12 x 12 inches and will hold exactly 1 cubic foot. Use ¾-inch plywood, exterior grade. You will need a handful of 8-penny common nails, scrap 1 x 2 or strapping, wood glue and urethane varnish for a smooth, tough finish, and bright paint or waterproof marker.

1. Cut 2 pieces of plywood 12 inches by 13½ inches; cut 2 more pieces 12 inches by 12 inches. Cut 2 lengths of 1 x 2 each 20 inches long.
2. Mark horizontal lines every 2⅖ inches on the interior of one side. (The inside edge of the tongue of a framing square is graduated in tenths; use this tool to lay out these lines.) Color each line with a marker or bright paint. Let the paint or marker dry.
3. Glue and nail the box together with the 12-inch-by-12-inch sides butting against the inside faces of the 12-inch-by-13½-inch sides as illustrated.
4. Glue and nail on the 1 x 2 handles.
5. Finish the box inside and out with several protective coats of urethane varnish.

The painted graduations each represent 20 percent, or ⅕ of the box's volume. (If you think quarter graduations will be more useful to you, mark the interior lines every 3 inches.)

Bottomless Measuring Box

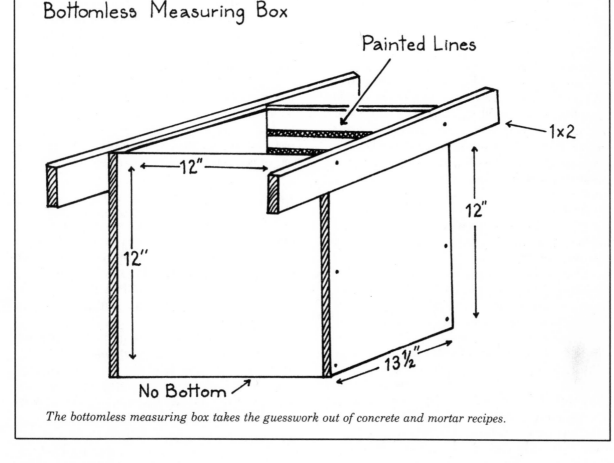

Painted Lines

1x2

12"

12"

12"

13½"

No Bottom

The bottomless measuring box takes the guesswork out of concrete and mortar recipes.

Sand and Water

Concrete and mortar recipes that include a water measurement are usually based on dry sand as a major ingredient. However, sand is rarely delivered dry, but is dampened by the dealer to keep it from blowing about and sifting away during transport. The damper the sand, the less water will be needed in the concrete or mortar mix. Studies show that if a mix recipe calls for 6 gallons of water to 1 sack of cement

Sand Wetness - Squeeze Sand
1. Barely Damp
2. Average
3. Very Wet

A simple observational squeeze test tells you how damp your sand is before you mix mortar.

and 3 cubic feet of sand, and the sand is of average dampness, only 5 gallons of water should be added. If the sand is really wet, the water requirement slips down to 4¼ gallons. For this reason, concrete and mortar recipes rarely specify a set amount of water. If you buy a bag of pre-mixed mortar cement and plan to follow the suggested additions of water and sand, test the sand's dampness first so that you don't weaken the mix by having it too wet. Pick up a handful of sand and squeeze it, then open your hand and examine it.

> *Barely damp:* the sand crumbles apart
> *Average dampness:* the sand clumps together in one mass
> *Very wet:* the sand clumps together and leaves much water on your palm

Reduce the amount of water the recipe calls for accordingly.

When you order sand, let the dealer know you want it for masonry work or for concrete work. Concrete sand is fairly coarse, while masonry sand is fine for greater plasticity and handling ease. Silt, clay and loam content in the sand can hurt the quality and strength of the finished concrete or mortar. Beach sand is terrible—the salts in it weaken concrete and mortar and prevent them from setting properly.

Any drinking water is usually fine for concrete or mortar work, though water with a high sulfate content is injurious to the bonding process. Salt water weakens concrete and mortar.

Mixing It Up

Store your bags of mix or cement in a *dry* protected place. Everyone has seen dank old storage sheds with one or two solid pillows of rain- or damp-set cement in the corner. Always wear gloves when you mix and work with concrete and mortar—both irritate and dry out skin severely.

The metal wheelbarrow, a mason's hoe with holes in it (or a plain old garden hoe) and elbow grease are the basics of the traditional way to mix a small batch of concrete or mortar. A deep wheelbarrow will hold a cubic foot of mix comfortably. The wheelbarrow has the added advantage of mobility—the load can be trundled along and brought close to the section of wall being laid. The mixing platform is a poor second best for garden and backyard structural work. If you use a wheelbarrow, *be sure to clean it out thoroughly before the mortar sets*. I can remember well my grandfather's cement-stucco wheelbarrow; it was an enervating shade of dull grey, had an extremely lumpy, coarse texture, and weighed about 300 pounds empty. A mixing tub or trough can be useful for larger jobs such as patio foundations or footings.

Mixing Mortar

1. Add the dry ingredients (including any damp sand) to the wheelbarrow and mix them together thoroughly with the hoe until their color is uniform. Scrape the dry ingredients to one end of the barrow, and at the other end pour in about half the water you think the mix will need.

2. Hoe the dry mix into the water and work back and forth, adding water *slowly and carefully* until the mix is of the right consistency and thickness. The less water you use, the stronger the mix; the more water, the weaker the end result.

Mixing Concrete

Add the cement and sand and mix them well, then add the aggregate stones and mix them thoroughly into the cement-sand combination. Drag the mix to one side and proceed to add water as for the mortar mix.

Hoe Dry Mix into Water

Dry Mix

Water

The traditional way to mix a small batch of concrete or mortar; it's important to clean the wheelbarrow out thoroughly before the mortar or concrete sets.

How to Tell When It's Ready

The hardest part for the first-time mason is deciding when the concrete or mortar has reached the proper consistency, but after you've worked with it for an hour you'll have a good idea of what the ideal body is like.

Concrete will be somewhat stiff but not crumbly, with just enough plasticity to allow you to get it into the corners of the forms and trenches, to fill all the crevices and to level it out under a screed without roughing up the surface. Concrete should not pour or flow fluidly, but move rather in a series of thick plops.

Mortar will be wetter and more plastic. It will roll evenly off the trowel when you throw a line, neither dribbling nor splattering—not fall off in one sluggish lump. With experience your skills will improve immeasurably.

Using the Mix

When you are working with concrete and mortar, especially when you are laying bricks, mix up the material a little now and then to keep it moist and in good working condition. You may have to add a tiny bit of water occasionally if the sun or wind is drying out the exposed surface.

If the weather turns cold before you get your project done, don't try to work with mortar once the temperature drops into the thirties; you run the risk of having the mortar freeze before it sets.

Always use mortar up within 2½ hours from the time you mix it, or you will find yourself cleaving futilely at a rigid, uncooperative mass.

Cover the top of the wall or structure with plastic to keep it dry if your work is interrupted by nightfall or more pressing affairs. Dew, frost and rain will add harmful moisture to the surface.

Helpful Sources for Beginning Masons

Donald R. Brann, *Bricklaying Simplified,* Directions Simplified, Easi-Bild Pattern Co., Briarcliff Manor, N.Y. 1971.

Louis M. Dezettel, *Masons and Builders Library: Bricklaying; Plastering; Rock Masonry; Clay Tile,* Theodore Audel and Co., Indianapolis, Ind., 1972, 1978.

Masonry, Time-Life Books, Alexandria, Va., 1976.

Basic Masonry Illustrated, Sunset-Lane Publishing Co., Menlo Park, Calif., 1981.

RAILROAD TIES

Be very careful with railroad ties around the garden. The creosote they were soaked in long ago is still toxic to your plants. One gardener in New Jersey has figured out a way around this problem. He made several large raised beds 16 feet long and 6 feet wide with walls of railroad ties stacked, drilled and secured to each other with steel pipe driven through the drilled holes. The interior walls were lined with black plastic (perforated for drainage) to prevent any contact of the plant roots with the creosoted ties. For a number of years he has grown vegetables and flowers of amazing robustness in these beds with no trace of creosote damage.

Railroad ties are not as easy to get now as they were only a few years ago, for a powerful machine called a tie cutter which runs along railroad tracks now literally bites the old ties into splintered halves so that they are useless to everybody. But in some regions of the country where technological progress has not reared its destructive head, you can still buy ties cheaply from the railroad. Many of the old ties were made of chestnut and were hand-hewn, the marks of the axe still on them.

Their massive forms make ties difficult to use in a small or wildflower garden, but in a larger setting they are a versatile material and can be used as risers and edging in a gravel path, as bed edging or raised bed containers (if backed with black plastic), as retaining walls and as low bumper walls to set off a parking area or to delineate one section of grounds from another. One of the problems with railroad ties is that enthusiastic gardeners who find a cheap supply tend to overdo things and end up with a garden that resembles a spur of the Union Pacific. When ties are used in retaining walls, as they often are, the heavy, brooding face of the wall should be softened with trees, shrubs and vines.

Getting Railroad Ties

Taken-up ties are usually hauled to a central point on the railroad line, stacked and sold. To find out when and where ties are available call the local railroad office. Sometimes the ties are thrown in the bushes beside the tracks. Smashed ties ruined by the new tie cutter are burned by railroad personnel along the tracks.

Transportation of the ties from the depot to your property is up to you. They are heavy, as much as 9 inches thick and up to 10 feet long. A local trucking firm can transport them for you, or you can carry a few in the back of a pickup truck. In 1982, rural trucking costs averaged about a dollar a mile.

Creosoted ties will last many decades in contact with the soil—up to 50 years or longer for treated *and* naturally rot-resistant timber.

If you saw a railroad tie into lengths, the exposed wood may not be as rot resistant as the uncut tie. Paint the exposed wood with a preservative non-injurious to plants (see chapter 2, "Fence Posts").

Building Walls with Railroad Ties

The basic principle of working with ties is the same as that of working with stone or brick—one-on-two, two-on-one for solid, interlocking strength. Ties are held together and set into the earth with steel pipe connectors.

1. The bottom tie of a wall should be set into the earth 3 or 4 inches. Prepare a level trench after marking the line of the wall with mason's twine stretched tautly between two stakes at ground level, then sprinkled with damp sand and lifted to leave a straight mark in the sand.

2. Drill the ends of each tie in the bottom row with holes large enough to receive ½-inch pipe.

3. Cut lengths of ½-inch pipe 2½ feet long. Insert the pipe lengths through the drilled holes with the ties in place, and hammer connectors deep into the ground until they are flush with the tie surface.

4. Set the second course of ties so that no joints are directly over others. Drill through the upper tie and several inches into the tie below it. Hammer pipe or reinforcing rod into the stacked ties through the drill hole until it is flush with the surface of the upper tie. 12-inch pipe sections will go through a 9-inch tie and penetrate 3 inches into the tie below it. Connect

Step 1. Dig Trench

9"   ↕ 3"

Step 2. Drill Bottom Row of Ties

Hole for ½" Pipe

Heavy-Duty Drill

Step 3. Hammer Pipe into Ground

Recess Pipe

Step 4. Set Second Course   Tie Courses Together

Anchor Pipes   Anchor Spikes

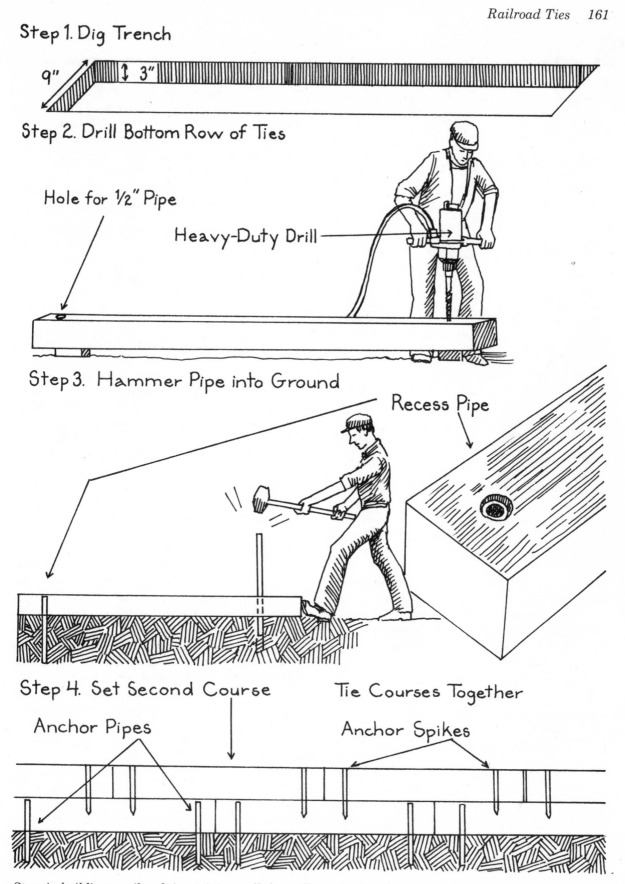

Steps in building a railroad tie retaining wall that will stay in place.

End View of Deadmen

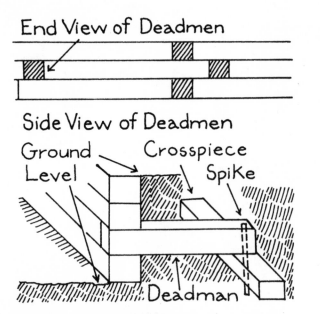

Side View of Deadmen

Deadmen tie a retaining wall securely into the earth and prevent the face of the wall from bulging outward and eventually collapsing.

each section of railroad tie to the course below it with pipe or rod at each end.

If you plan a retaining wall higher than 3 feet, you will have to anchor it with deadmen—but first check the building code for your town to find out the specifications for such a structure.

Deadmen

Ties make good retaining walls *if* they are tied into the backfill with deadmen. A deadman is a timber set at right angles to the wall and extending back into the earth as much as 4 feet. A 4 x 4 crosspiece should be bolted on the earth end of the deadman before the fill is dumped onto the timbers. Each deadman is thus a powerful anchor that holds the wall in place. A railroad tie retaining wall of any height above

2 or 3 feet without deadmen is dangerous, possibly bulging outward and collapsing in time.

Old telephone poles—which may cost several dollars per foot—can be used in retaining walls and as dividers in the same way as railroad ties. Check with your telephone business office for local supplies and prices.

Constructing Railroad Tie Steps

A gravel or shredded bark path through a woodland garden or on sloping ground can be made into an easier, pleasanter walkway by breaking steep sections into long, gently sloped steps with railroad tie risers which also hold the soil in place.

1. Measure the degree of slope (see chapter 2, "Fence Posts") in the section you want to modify, measure the length of the path and work out on paper the graduated length and slope of each step before you set shovel to earth. Mark the ground with mason's twine and stakes.

2. Dig out each step and level the earth firmly with a 4 x 4 tamper. Set aside some soil for backfill, and allow room for 1 inch of gravel or bark fill to come flush with the surface of the railroad tie riser after the backfill has been added.

3. Cut and drill the ties to take 2½-foot lengths of ½-inch pipe at each end. Hammer in the pipe until it is flush with the tie surface, then countersink it slightly with another section of pipe and a hammer. Set all the ties firmly in place before backfilling if you like.

4. Backfill behind each tie with soil, firmly tamping down the layers. The top layer should be 1 inch of gravel or shredded bark level with the surface of the tie. After a few weeks the topping will have settled and should be brought up to the tie level again by adding more material.

Steps in a Gravel Path

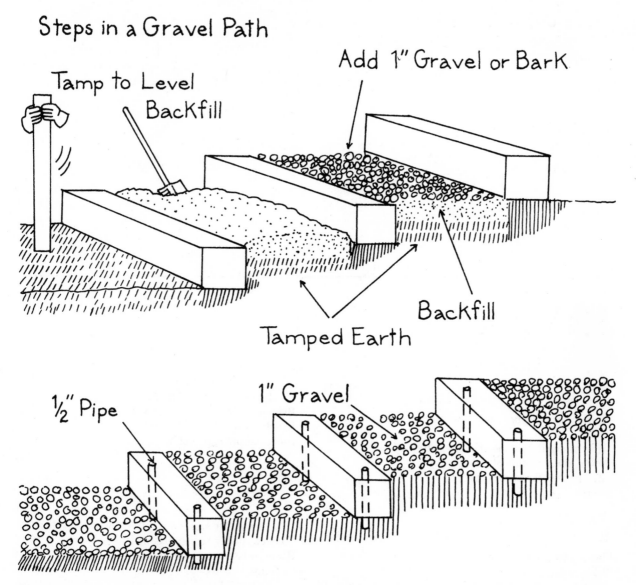

Tamp to Level

Backfill

Add 1" Gravel or Bark

Tamped Earth

Backfill

½" Pipe

1" Gravel

Pipe sections hammered into the ground will anchor railroad tie steps in place. A loose tie section that simply lies on the ground is very soon dislodged and askew and becomes an impediment to the garden stroller rather than an aid. If you do not want to bother with the labor of drilling ties and setting pipe, an alternate way of securing ties is to drive rot-resistant hardwood pegs into the earth along the bottom front edge. This will give you a few years of secure ties.

Mail-Order Sources for
Post Hole Digging Tools and Stone Mason's Tools

Farm Catalog
Sears, Roebuck & Co.
925 South Doman Avenue
Chicago, IL 60607

Dana Farm Supplies
Hyde Park, VT 05655

NASCO Farm Supplies
1524 Princeton Avenue
Modesto, CA 95352

Berstein Brothers, Inc.
100 North Mechanic Street
Pueblo, CO 81003

Forestry Suppliers, Inc.
205 West Rankin Street
Box 8397
Jackson, MS 39204

Ben Meadows Co.
3589 Broad Street
Atlanta (Chamblee), GA 30366

Farm Catalog
Montgomery Ward
619 West Chicago Avenue
Chicago, IL 60607

INDEX